Sexual Life
in Ancient Egypt

Fayence figurine.
Private collection in Denmark.

Sexual Life
in Ancient Egypt

Lise Manniche

KEGAN PAUL INTERNATIONAL
LONDON AND NEW YORK

First published in 1987 by
Kegan Paul International
UK: P.O. Box 256, London WC1B 3SW, England
Tel: (0171) 580 5511 Fax: (0171) 436 0899
E-mail: books@keganpau.demon.co.uk
Internet: http://www.demon.co.uk/keganpaul/
USA: 562 West 113th Street, New York, NY 10025, USA
Tel: (212) 666 1000   Fax: (212) 316 3100

First paperback edition 1997

Distributed by

John Wiley & Sons Ltd
Southern Cross Trading Estate
1 Oldlands Way, Bognor Regis
West Sussex, PO22 9SA, England
Tel: (01243) 779 777   Fax: (01243) 820 250

Columbia University Press
562 West 113th Street
New York, NY 10025, USA
Tel: (212) 666 1000   Fax: (212) 316 3100

Printed in Great Britain by Redwood Books

British Library Cataloguing in Publication Data

Manniche, Lise
    Sexual life in ancient Egypt
    1. Sex customs – Egypt – History   2. Egyptians – Sexual
    behavior – History   3. Erotica – Egypt   4. Egypt – Social life
    and customs – to 332 B.C.
    I. Title
    306.7'0932

    ISBN 0710305516

Library of Congress Cataloguing-in-Publication Data

Manniche, Lise
    Sexual life in ancient Egypt / Lise Manniche. – 1st paperback ed.
        p. cm.
    Includes bibliographical references and index.
    ISBN 0-7103-0551-6 (pbk.)
    1. Sex customs – Egypt – History   2. Egypt – Social life and
    customs – to 332 B.C.   3. Erotica – History   I. Title
    HQ13.M36   1996
    306.7'0932 – dc20
                                                        96–16781
                                                             CIP

Contents

Introduction

Judging from the books available on erotic life in the Ancient World, the Greeks and Romans would appear to be pioneers in the field of describing and, especially, depicting this aspect of human behaviour. This may be so in some respects, but others had prepared the ground. Along the banks of the Nile erotic life flourished at all levels of society and, contrary to what is generally thought, it was recorded in words and pictures.

Evidence on any subject concerned with ancient Egypt is almost always fragmentary, but information about the intimate life of the inhabitants is particularly scarce. What is known about life in those distant days has been gathered mainly from tombs and temples and is therefore, to a large extent, of a funerary or religious nature. Few urban settlements have survived but it is, in fact, remains of such agglomerations of buildings which have yielded the most interesting vestiges of the intimate life of the people who lived there.

When attempting to piece together a picture of the sexual behaviour of the Egyptians during the 3000 years or so before Christ one is further hampered by the fact that whenever 'erotic' drawings and figurines have had the good fortune to survive the millennia, they frequently ended up in private collections or in inaccessible drawers in museums.

The sources include representations in the round, reliefs, paintings and, above all, sketches of erotic scenes. Texts vividly describe the passions and desires of gods and men. The belief in a life in the Hereafter was all important to the Egyptians and it was emphasized in the tangible concept of the act of procreation preceding it. In the same way as the union of male and female was a necessity for the creation of a new being, this underlying erotic force also enabled a person who had departed from this life to go on existing in the Hereafter. The sexual power of the mummy had to be maintained and stimulated. This is always visualized as pertaining to the mummy of a man, never that of a woman. In Egyptian art the idea is expressed in a symbolic way which is quite straightforward once the coded language is understood; it can be seen to permeate scenes and subjects which are generally taken at their face value only.

The literary sources are fairly uncomplicated. There are tales of the conflicts of gods and the adventures of men, and love poems written in a simple language but with numerous *double entendres* and play on words. Wisdom books advise how to behave towards fellow human beings and to women in particular; calendars suggest activities to be abstained from on certain days of the year; dream books give the solution to the subconscious adventures of men and women; and magic formulas make everything come true.

When reading these ancient writings and perceiving how the Egyptians attempted to make their erotic visions last by putting pen to paper or chisel to stone, one is hardly aware of the gap in time and cultural tradition which is otherwise most acutely felt when trying to understand how the Egyptian mind worked.

The Attitude of the Egyptians to Sex

Herodotus, the Greek historian and traveller to Egypt in the 5th century BC, was the first foreigner to try to bridge this gap in understanding by telling the world about the Egyptians of his time and, insofar as possible, of their ancestors. He collected extensive information about this strange people. He was concerned with almost any kind of information and he passed on whatever he heard, leaving it to the reader to believe it or not. We are still wondering how much of it was actually true.

Among the more intimate details concerning the Egyptians he obtained the following piece of information, apparently a mixture of what he had himself observed and what he had been told.

> The women urinate in a standing position, whereas the men sit down. They relieve themselves indoors and eat in the street, and they give as reason for this the fact that things unseemly should be performed in private, but things not unseemly should be done in the open. The Egyptians and those who have learnt it from them are the only ones to perform circumcision. Every man has two garments, every woman just one. They are particularly careful always to wear clean linen. They circumcise for reasons of cleanliness more than seemliness. Their priests shave their bodies every second day, so that no lice nor any other pollution should contaminate them in the service of the god. . . . They wash with cold water twice during the day and twice during the night. (II. 35–7)[1]

On this occasion Herodotus had nothing more to say about anything remotely connected with sexual matters (but he refers to them later, cf. below). One may perhaps take it however, that erotic activities were among those which took place indoors (or he would

1. Circumcision. Tomb of Ankhmahor, Saqqara. Early 6th dyn.

have noticed and not omitted commenting on it) and therefore considered by the Egyptians to be, if not 'unseemly', at least fairly private.

9

Introduction

The Egyptians appreciated personal cleanliness both in daily life and in ritual circumstances, as Herodotus had observed. About the question of sexual matters being considered impure he adds: 'The Egyptians were the first to make it a matter of religious observance not to have intercourse with women in temples nor to enter a temple without washing after being with a woman.' (II. 64) This is the only suggestion that intimate relations with women were considered unclean as compared with the ritually pure condition required of a person entering a holy place, a concept which is by no means alien to the present-day descendants of the ancient Egyptians now devoted to Islam. Long before Herodotus intercourse in temples was thought best to avoid. In *The Book of the Dead*, which most wealthy Egyptians arranged to have placed in their tombs close to the mummy, there is a list of actions which the deceased was supposed to swear not to have committed. In order to be allowed to dwell in the kingdom of Osiris, his conscience should permit him to stand up and declare: 'I have not committed adultery in the sacred places of my city god.' (P. Nu, ch. 125, Introd., 12)[2]

Some women had a special part to play in the presence of the god and aggressive sexual behaviour was even encouraged for they had to stimulate the virility of the god. Diodorus, the historian who visited Egypt in 60–57 BC, describes what happened after the funeral of the sacred Apis bull when the new bull was to be installed:

... Putting it on a state barge fitted out with a gilded cabin, they conduct it as a god to the sanctuary of Hephaestus at Memphis. During ... forty days only women may look at it; these stand facing it, and pulling up their garments show their genitals, but henceforth they are forever prevented from coming into the presence of this god. (I. 85)[3]

According to Herodotus a similar display took place during the festival of the cat-goddess Bastet:

When the people are on their way to Bubastis [to worship Artemis, i.e., Bastet] they go by river, men and women together, a great number of each in every boat. Some of the women make a noise with *krotala* (rattles), others play *auloi* (pipes) all the way, while the rest of the women, and the men, sing and clap their hands. As they journey by river to Bubastis, whenever they come near any town they bring their boat near the bank; then some of the women do as I have said, while some shout mocking of the women of the town, others dance, and others stand up and expose their persons. This they do whenever they come beside any riverside town. But when they have reached Bubastis, they make a festival with great sacrifices, and more wine is drunk at this feast than in the whole year beside. (II. 60)

10

2. *Terracotta figurine of man
showing his private parts.
British Museum.*

This aggressive behaviour of the women, reflected in numerous Graeco-Roman terracotta figurines, is probably the feminine equivalent of the cases in which men use their virility to gain power over another person, as we shall see later on.

Another aspect of the concept of the physical needs of the god was the offering of phallic votive gifts which, eventually, were to benefit the supplicant himself. The Egyptians placed phallic objects in the temple of Hathor, goddess of love, or figurines of Bes, the dwarf god, with a disproportionately large member. Herodotus relates what happened at the feast of Dionysos:

> The . . . festival of Dionysos is ordered by the Egyptians much as it is by the Greeks, except for the dances; but in place of the phallus they have invented the use of puppets a cubit long moved by strings, which are carried about the villages by women, the male member moving and nearly as big as the rest of the body; a pipe-player goes before, the women follow after, singing of Dionysos. There is a sacred legend which gives the reason for the appearance and motions of these puppets. (II. 48)

The legend to which Herodotus makes reference is probably the legend of Isis and Osiris. Osiris was once king of the living, but his brother Seth killed him, cut his body into pieces and scattered them over Egypt. Isis, the wife of Osiris, patiently collected them, but

> the only part of Osiris which Isis did not find was his male member; for no sooner had it been thrown into the river than it was swallowed by the *lepidotus,* the *phagrus* and the *oxyrrhyncus* fish . . . . In its place Isis shaped a dummy and consecrated the phallus to whose honour the Egyptians celebrate a feast to this day.[4]

This version of the well-known legend was written by Plutarch about AD 120. According to another tradition the missing part was found after all. The Egyptians never worshipped the phallus as such, but the existence of numerous figurines, particularly of Graeco-Roman date, is evidently inspired by this tradition.

Prostitution

In various places in the Middle East, in Greece and in India there was a particular arrangement intended for the pleasure of gods and men: temple prostitution. It is difficult to determine the extent to which this had a place in Egypt. There were priestesses of different rank in the temples, some even bearing the title of 'god's wife', or, referring to one of the creation legends, 'hand of the god', but this does not necessarily mean that they had sexual intercourse with the gods or with the priests in their place. Herodotus says explicitly:

3. Phallic figure carried in procession. Saqqara.

4. Wall-painting in the tomb of Neferhotep (No. 49) at Thebes. 18th dyn.

'There is a woman who sleeps in the temple of the Theban Jupiter [the temple of Amun], and it is reported that these women have no intercourse with any man.' (I. 182) When Strabo, the geographer, travelled in Egypt some 500 years later in 25 BC customs must have changed, for he was otherwise informed:

14

To Zeus [Amun] they consecrate one of the most beautiful girls of the most illustrious family. . . . She becomes a prostitute and has intercourse with whoever she wishes, until the purification of her body [menstruation] takes place. After her purification she is given in marriage to a man, but before the marriage and after her time as a prostitute, a ceremony of mourning is celebrated in her honour. (XVII. 1, 46)[5]

In one of his manifestations the god Amun was depicted with an erect phallus and he was reported to have had his own harem. But whether any of his ladies had anything but symbolic intercourse with him remains an open question.

There is more unambiguous proof of prostitution at a non-religious level. The literary sources tell of women who could be had for money; archaeological evidence points to the same conclusion. There are, for example, numerous documents from the workmen's village of Deir el-Medina telling of women who were neither wives nor mothers, but belonged with 'the others'. The inhabitants of the village by the end of the second millennium BC consisted, as far as the men are

5. *Ostrakon from Deir el-Medina, Cairo IFAO 3650. New Kingdom.*

6. *Wall-painting from a house at Deir el-Medina. 19th dyn.*

concerned, of stonemasons, draughtsmen and painters who decorated the tombs in the Valley of Kings on the other side of the mountain. They took turns of ten days in the Valley and this constant flow of men coming and going must have left its impression on the morale of the village. Fragments of legal texts tell of adultery and abortions and a whole section of the necropolis appears to have been meant for women alone or with their children. The wives and mothers were buried with the men in the family sepulchres.

The workmen in the village liked to draw sketches on flakes of limestone which abounded at the foot of the hill. They used these 'note pads' for drawing illustrations of fables and tales, or pictures of scenes to be painted in the tombs, or episodes from their daily life, including perhaps some wishful thinking: the songstress with the heavy wig, resting on her lute, and wearing hardly anything; or ladies in intimate situations in their bedroom or in circumstances which must have been a direct result of the liberal attitude in the village: in the birth chamber, with toddlers, midwives and other women around. The itinerant musicians and acrobats were also

7. *Ostrakon from Deir el-Medina, Cairo IFAO 3000. New Kingdom.*

depicted, easily recognizable because of the tattoo on the thigh, often featuring Bes who was the protector of anything to do with the private life of a woman. Perhaps the tattoo was meant as a protection against venereal disease like gonorrhoea which seems to have been known in ancient times, as distinct from syphilis which was not.

At Abydos in Middle Egypt there was another cemetery for women and children of the Ramessid period. The women were songstresses of the god and only one of them is buried with her husband. From ancient times Abydos was a cult centre where pilgrims arrived from all parts of the country. Wherever there is an influx of foreigners, this particular kind of institution tends to emerge, as exemplified in the presence of the cemeteries at Deir el-Medina and Abydos.

A couple of hundred years BC a story was told concerning Isis who was fleeing with her son Horus. At a certain point she needed shelter for the night and knocked on the door of a house which can only have been one of the pleasure houses of those days.

> At last I got to the house of the prostitutes. As soon as the Lady had seen me from afar, she closed her door to me. This annoyed my companions [seven scorpions]. They deliberated on it and put their poison together on the sting of Tefenet [one of them]. A harlot opened her door to me, and we entered the shabby dwelling. But Tefenet had crept under the door and stung the son of the Lady. A fire broke out in the house, and there was no water with which to put it out. The skies rained into the house of the Lady although it was not its season. Because she had not opened her door to me, she was distressed and she did not know whether her son would live. She walked about the town and cried, but no one heeded her cries. (Socle Béhague, Spell I)[6]

8. *Ostrakon from Deir el-Medina, Cairo IFAO 3779. 19th dyn.*

Eventually, Isis cured the Lady's son with her magic. The interpretation of this text lies entirely in the translation of the words here rendered by 'Lady', 'prostitute' and 'harlot'. The latter two occur elsewhere in a context which makes this translation fairly likely.

Herodotus was told some anecdotes of women who sold their bodies of their own free will, or more or less so.

> King Rhampsinitus bade his daughter to sit in a certain room and receive all alike who came; before she had intercourse with any, she should compel him to tell her what was the cleverest trick and the greatest crime of his life. (II. 121)

The purpose of this was for the king to find a certain thief.

10. Ostrakon in a private collection.

19

King Cheops who built the greatest pyramid in Egypt for himself had an equally bad reputation among the informants of Herodotus:

> And so evil a man was Cheops that for the lack of money he made his own daughter sit in a chamber and exact payment (how much I know not; for they did not tell me this). She, they say, doing her father's bidding, was minded to leave some memorial of her own, and demanded of everyone who sought intercourse with her that he should give her one stone to set in her work; and of these stones were built the pyramid that stand midmost of the three, over against the great pyramid; each side of it measures 150 feet. (II. 126)

Concubines and Adultery

Although prostitution was a well-established aspect of erotic behaviour, it was something which the Egyptians themselves condemned, particularly if married persons were involved. If a married woman committed adultery, she might lose her life or, in Graeco-Roman times, get away with divorce. Nevertheless, there are numerous examples from literature to show that it did occur, if not in actual fact then at least in the form of swearing to the opposite. A man called Amenemhet had a slab engraved telling of his irreproachable behaviour. Among other things it says: 'I was a priest, the "stick of old age" at his father's side, while he was yet among the living. . . . I did not know the slave girl in his house. I did not seduce his maid servant.'[7] And another man writes in a letter to his departed wife:

> I did not cause you any pain as to what I did as your master; you never saw me deceiving you like a peasant, going to another house. . . . Look, I have spent three years on my own without going to another house, although it is by no means suitable to be obliged to do so. But look, I did it for your sake. Look, as concerns the women in the house, I did not have intercourse with them. (P. Leiden 37, 1.18–20, 35–7, 38)[8]

To 'go to another house' presumably had a rather definite erotic sense.

To have a mistress while being yet unmarried was another matter and apparently quite legitimate. Around 2000 BC a man called Hekanakhte wrote the following letter to his family while he was away on business:

> I said to you: 'Do not keep away a companion of Hetepet's from her, whether her hair-dresser or her domestic servant(?).' Take great care of her. May you prosper in all things thus. Now (if) you do not want her, then you should send Iutenheb to me. As this man lives for me – I speak of Ip – he who shall commit any act upon the person (?) of (my) concubine (Hetepet) he is against me and I am against him. See! Whoever will do

11. *Ostrakon from el-Amarna. 18th dyn.*

for her the like of what I have done – Indeed, would any of you be patient if his wife had been denounced to him? Then shall I be patient! How can I be with you in the same establishment? No! You will not respect (my) concubine for my sake. (II. 38–44)[9]

The concubine is to have the same status as a legal wife. This may have been the exception to the rule. On the other hand there is archaeological evidence which suggests that, contrary to what the texts declare to be the norm, a married man could have a concubine, even if his legal wife had been able to bear children. The governor of one of the provinces in Middle Egypt near the modern village of Beni Hasan, who was roughly contemporary with Hekanakhte, appears to have had a concubine who became treasurer in the household and eventually married the governor, presumably after the death of his first wife. While she was still a concubine she bore him two sons and a daughter.

Another mistress regrets being thrown out and replaced:

It is like a cross-eyed woman who has lived for twenty years in the house of a man; but then he finds another woman and says to her: 'I repudiate you, for you are cross-eyed!' And she replies: 'Because you have not found out during the twenty years I have lived in your house, I am the one who is mocking you!.' (P. Bibl. Nat. 198)[10]

To 'find another' was an expression used among lovers who were not legally married. In Graeco-Roman times it became a legal term for adultery.

Herodotus was told of how difficult it was to find a woman who had been faithful to her husband:

> When he [a son of Ramesses II] had been blind for ten years an oracle from the city of Buto declared to him that the time of his punishment was drawing to an end, and that he should regain his sight by washing his eyes with the issue of a woman who had never had intercourse with any man but her own husband. Pheros made a trial with his own wife first, and he still remained blind (although he tried) with all women, one after the other. When at last he recovered sight he took all the women of whom he had made trial, save only her who had made him see again, and gathered them into one town, that which is now called Red Clay; where having collected them together he burnt them and the town; but the woman by whose means he had recovered sight he took to wife. (II. 111)

Homosexuality

In theory a number of variations in sexual behaviour were not alien to the Egyptians, but again the sources are most discreet as to what actually took place. As far as homosexuality is concerned there are but few examples to suggest that it was indulged in for pleasure. Raping another man was an act of aggression, a means of gaining power over an adversary. A passage in *The Book of the Dead* speaks of it as a virtue not to have committed a homosexual act, and a list of prohibitions valid in various cities suggests the same. A much discussed passage in one of the wisdom texts points to the same attitude. Pictorial evidence is ambiguous. In some of the sketches showing two persons in an intimate situation it is difficult to distinguish the sex of the participants. There is an allusion in a tale in which the god Seth, whose bi-sexual inclinations are evident elsewhere, jumps at the goddess Anat who is a sort of Amazon, dressed as a man.

Homosexuality among women is even more sparsely documented. In a *Book of the Dead* written for a woman it says: 'I have not had intercourse with any woman in the sacred places of my city god,'[11] but beyond doubt the text was copied from a 'male' version and an obvious mistake has not been corrected. But the possibility had, nevertheless, entered some people's minds, for in a dream book for women it is said: 'If she dreams that a woman has intercourse with her, she will come to a bad end.' (P. Carlsberg XIII, b2, 33)[12]

12. *Wall-painting from a Theban tomb, British Museum 37981. 18th dyn.*

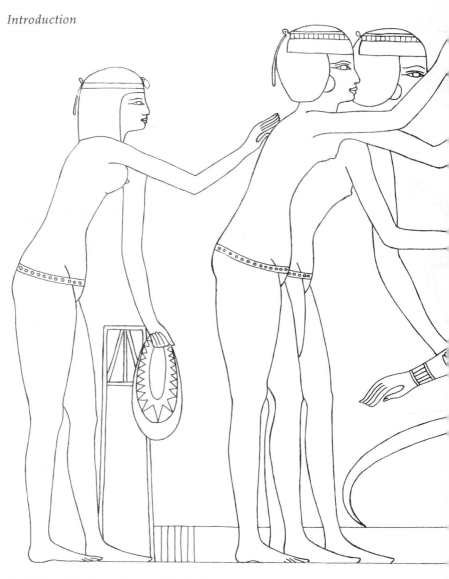

13. *Wall-painting from the tomb of Ptahemhet (No. 77) at Thebes (from drawing by Prisse d'Avennes). 18th dyn.*

Without exactly accusing them of being lesbians it is obvious that women enjoyed being touched by other women. A mother is shown kissing her teenage daughter on the mouth, or the ladies at a banquet embrace each other and show erotic symbols to one another.

24

In the period of Egyptian history called the Amarna Period the difference between the sexes appears to be almost obliterated. Men and women of the upper circles imitate the royal couple and wear identical loose garments, so thin and diaphanous that they reveal

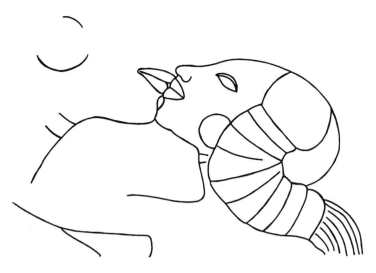

14. *Relief from el-Amarna, The Brooklyn Museum, New York 60.197.8. 18th dyn.*

that the ideal image of the body underneath was virtually the same for men and women. It is the male image adapting to the female. King Akhnaten depicts himself in the image of his wife Nefertiti with small firm breasts, narrow waist and heavily rounded hips and thighs. As Nefertiti sometimes wears diadems and crowns it is often

15. *Wall-painting in the tomb of Haremhab (No. 78) at Thebes (from Hay MSS 29823, 10). 18th dyn.*

16. *Stela from el-Amarna, Ägyptisches Museum, East Berlin 17813. 18th dyn.*

difficult to tell the difference between the two. There was probably a well-defined ideology behind these iconographical peculiarities. Possibly the king regarded himself as the male and female principles united in his own creative person.

Intercourse with Animals

Herodotus was shocked by the sexual relations between men and animals in Egypt. 'In my lifetime a monstrous thing happened in this province, a woman having open intercourse with a he-goat. This came to be publicly known.' (II. 46) The province in question was Mendes where the goat was sacred; what Herodotus witnessed was probably a ritual act, as when the virility of the Apis bull was strengthened by the women showing their private parts to it.

In the dream books there are various combinations of animals and men which show that these relationships existed in the erotic imagination of the Egyptians, if not in actual fact. Men may copulate with jerboas, swallows and pigs, whereas women have a choice between mouse, horse, donkey, ram, wolf, lion, crocodile, snake, baboon, ibis or falcon. Most frequently the dreams are an omen of bad fate.

When one Egyptian swore at another, he might use an expression which reflected a relationship which few women would favour: 'May a donkey copulate with your wife and children!'[13] It must have been an oath frequently used and long lived, for it may have provided the inspiration for a faience figurine depicting exactly this situation. Incidentally, the donkey was related to the god Seth who was particularly noted for his aggressive sexual behaviour.

Necrophilia

Certain rumours were caused by the habit of the Egyptians of having dead bodies made into mummies; it was reported that the embalmers abused the corpses of the most beautiful women. Again Herodotus was well informed:

> Wives of notable men, and women of great beauty and reputation, are not at once given over to the embalmers, but only after they have been dead three or four days; this is done that the embalmers may not have carnal intercourse with them. For it is said that one was found having intercourse with a woman newly dead, and was denounced by his fellow workmen. (II. 89)

Xenophon of Ephesus, another classic author, tells that a man kept the embalmed body of his wife in his bedroom, though it remains an open question why he did so. The physical remains of mummies sometimes show that they have been left for some time before being embalmed, as they are partly decomposed, but it may not be for the reason mentioned above. The Egyptian embalmers may have had a rather different attitude to corpses than their modern counterparts, for it was generally believed that a deceased person kept his sexual powers, as Osiris, king of the dead, had done, and he had even been able to produce an heir after his death. The sexual power of the dead was a significant factor not to be ignored. In the shape of a bird it could return to the land of the living and cause considerable damage.

Incest

The royal family of the last three centuries BC, of Greek descent, provided numerous examples of marriage between closely related persons, and for this reason Egypt has acquired a reputation of being almost the cradle of incest. This was supported by the very literal interpretation by the early Egyptologists of the words 'sister' and 'brother', used among lovers and married people.

In pharaonic Egypt incest was the exception, not the rule, but within the royal family special circumstances applied. For reasons of legitimacy a pharaoh might marry his half-sister, or perhaps one of his daughters, as did Ramesses II. Amenophis III may have had a relationship with one of his daughters, too, and, according to the way in which the evidence is interpreted, this may also have been the case with Akhnaten. King Seneferu of the Old Kingdom may have had offspring by his own daughter, and Herodotus heard how King Mycerinus had designs on his.

Among ordinary people marriage between closely related persons was by no means common (unregistered cases of incest of course remain unknown). Among the numerous liaisons which it has proved possible to investigate, there is only a single one which can be said to be incestuous; two are 'almost certain', two more are 'unlikely, but possible'. In all instances it was a question of half-sisters or half-brothers. On the basis of the available material it can therefore be ascertained that nothing suggests that incest was common among ordinary people in ancient Egypt.

Polygamy

Polygamy does not seem to have ever been in fashion. Whenever a man is known to have had several wives, nothing usually suggests that he had them at the same time. As adultery was generally con-demned, there is little to indicate that polygamy was a general rule. In the royal family it was different, for marriages were arranged with foreign princesses for political reasons. Polygamy seems to have been particularly common in the reign of Amenophis III when a number of foreign princesses came to the court of Egypt. Some of them even-tually had an impressive burial, for the jars which once contained their intestines have been found in the neighbourhood of the Valley of the Queens. The very imaginative names of these ladies suggest something about the part they once played in the king's harem: 'She of numerous nights in the city of the brilliant Aten'; 'She who appears in glory in the temple of the brilliant Aten'; 'She who strikes with fury for the brilliant Aten'.

Other Aspects of Sexual Life

The existence of one of the more unusual sexual activities is suggested by one source alone: a small fragment of a leather wall hanging(?) dating from about 1500 BC. It has a painted scene showing a girl playing the harp while a naked man with a most unrealistic phallus turned backwards dances to the music. In his left hand he holds an object which resembles, above all, a whip with several lashes. Other women are present in the arbour of gourds, for a foot and an ankle ring are visible on the extreme right. The leather hanging was found at Deir el-Bahari in Upper Egypt where Hathor, the goddess of love, had a shrine. Unfortunately, it is no longer possible to view this scene in its unexpurgated state. At the beginning of the present century the too-obvious phallus was erased and only an old photograph gives a clue to the significance of the scene.

17. *Leather hanging from Deir el-Bahari, Metropolitan Museum of Art, 31.3.98. 18th dyn.*

18. *Papyrus British Museum 10,018.*

In one of the creation legends it is described how the god of creation created the other gods with his hand, i.e., by masturbating. In another papyrus a variant to this account is depicted: the god uses his mouth instead of his hand. Whether this technique was in use among mortal men remains an open question.

The Erotic Language in Words and Pictures

In the following pages the Egyptians will speak through their tales of gods and men, and their poems and wisdom books. The language used varies a great deal in these source texts, partly because the genres of literature are different, partly because the texts span a couple of thousand years.

In the mythological tales and the factual books straightforward wording is employed. The Egyptians say exactly what they mean. In the love poems, on the other hand, and to a certain extent in the literary texts about human beings, play on words and *double entendres* are used, though many of these are undoubtedly lost to the modern reader and translator.

The Egyptians did not always speak in a polite manner. Some of their curses were inspired by sexual matters. There was no doubt, however, that, ideally, one should keep to a decent language: 'Your mouth does not fornicate,' or 'You have abstained from adulterous talk,' is recommended in a papyrus from the Ramessid Period *c.* 1000 BC (P. Lansing 14,8).[14] But in the Old Kingdom a thousand years earlier a man exclaims while fighting with another in a boat: 'Come on, you fornicator!' (Tomb of Ti)[15] It was apparently not thought unseemly to carve this challenging remark on the wall of a tomb which was, in a way, an official monument.

The word designating the female private parts was used in a deprecatory sense. A woman who has played a dirty trick on someone is called a ⸂𓏲𓈖⸃ *kat tahut, kat* meaning vulva and *tahut* presumably prostitute. Ramesses II used a related expression to describe submissive cowards:

31

. . . But when the cities had made no resistance and been easily taken, he put an inscription on the pillars even as he had done where the nations were brave, but he drew also on them the privy parts of a woman, wishing to show clearly that the people were cowardly. (Herodotus II. 102)

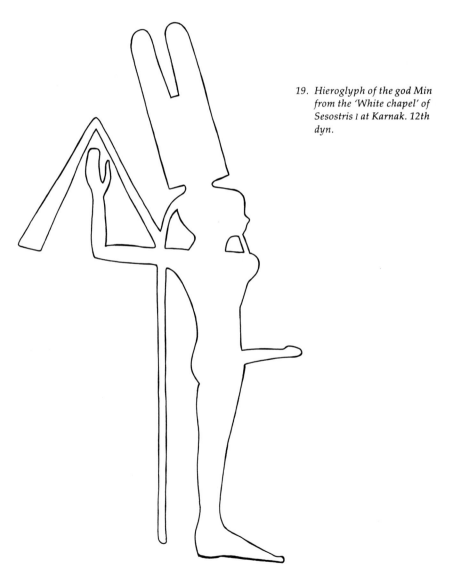

19. Hieroglyph of the god Min from the 'White chapel' of Sesostris I at Karnak. 12th dyn.

Whereas the word *kat* was used in anatomical description or in a deprecatory sense, the word ᴐ⁴ₑⁱⁱ *keniw* 'embrace' is used for the same part of a woman's body in a more poetical context. In a love poem the young man says 'She showed me the colour of her embrace,' the word 'colour' appearing to have an erotic connotation. Another poem mentions 'seeing the colour of all her limbs'. In the tale of the herdsman who saw a goddess in the meadows, he is enticed by her 'colour' which was so 'smooth'.

Being together in a sexual sense could be described in many ways.[16] Poetically it was called 'spending a pleasant hour together'. If the encounter took place outside the bonds of marriage, it might be phrased as 'entering a house'. But if a single word was required to describe the act, there were some twenty words to choose from. By far the most frequent in legal documents, wisdom books, calendars and dream books was ⩯⩰ *nek*, the root of which survives in modern Arabic. In literary texts the more neutral 'to know' was used. A different expression was the modern sounding 'to sleep with', 'to enjoy oneself with', 'to unite oneself with', and a whole series of words which must, until we grasp the finer points, simply be translated as 'having intercourse' or the like.

The Egyptians also had a word to describe the climax of the act. 'To ejaculate' was the simple way of describing what happened to the man, graphically illustrated in the hieroglyphic ⌐ₒ⩰⩯ but, judging from the last sign being repeated as a determinative for other expressions, it is quite likely that several of the words translated as 'having intercourse' describe the same stage of the proceedings. It cannot be proven beyond doubt whether female orgasm was acknowledged, but a few passages may be interpreted to this effect. In one of the wisdom texts it is explained how boring life becomes after the age of sixty when you can neither eat nor drink as before, and when 'you lust after a woman, her moment does not come.' In another text describing the union between the god Amun and a beautiful queen of Egypt, it appears that the queen cries out at the moment of climax.

Just as the Egyptians used pictorial expressions in their love language there existed a kind of code language within pictorial art. Some pictures may not need an explanation, but this only applies to 'unofficial' art as, for example, sketches and graffiti which have much in common with their modern counterparts. Other representations on the walls of tombs and temples imply a ritual or magical significance. The god Min, for instance, was depicted in his ithyphallic glory in relief and statuary. This was never considered indecent; the eye-catching attribute of the god was an essential part of his iconography. Apart from anything else the Egyptians were used to drawing phalloi for the simple reason that it was a frequently employed hieroglyph used to render a sound in words which had nothing to do with erotic matters at all.

In Egyptian art erotic scenes as such are extremely rare. A tiny little hieroglyph in a tomb of Middle Kingdom date shows a couple intimately linked on top of a bed. The sign has since been erased from the wall, but it was copied intact by the middle of the nineteenth century. The meaning of the hieroglyph in the text unfortunately remains cryptic and there is no large-scale representation to go with it.

20. *Painting on the ceiling in the tomb of*
    Ramesses IX in the Valley of the Kings.
    20th dyn.

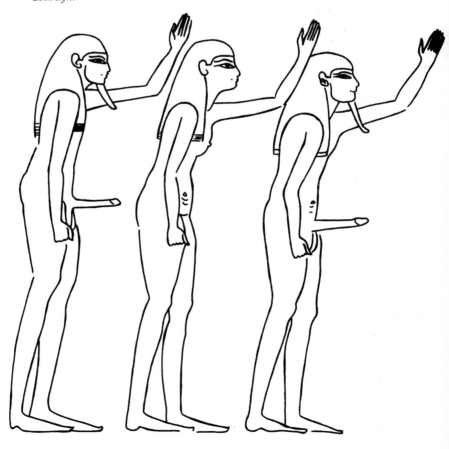

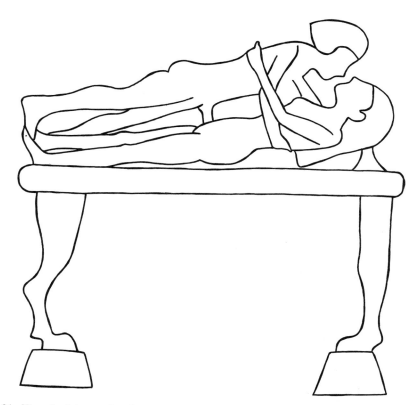

21. Hieroglyph in a tomb at Beni Hasan. Ca. 2000BC.

In a house dating from shortly before the Christian era a wall was adorned with several drawings of people having intercourse. Whether or not they were meant as graffiti or as a contribution to the general decor of the room it is tempting to see in them a pointer to the purpose of the building as a house of pleasure, and to compare it with remains of a number of rooms in a building of a slightly earlier date. At the beginning of the present century archaeologists uncovered at Saqqara four rooms of a mud-brick house of rather rough construction. Some of the rooms had brick benches along the walls; these latter were decorated with representations of the god Bes, 1–1½ metres high, covered with stucco and painted. As we shall see the dwarf god Bes is often present where physical love is celebrated. In addition, some thirty-two phallic figures were recovered from the debris. These 'Bes chambers' would appear either to have sheltered lady inmates and their clients or else to have been a place of worship for those who needed reassurance for reasons of procreation.

35

22. *Wall-paintings in a house at Hermopolis. 1st cent. BC.*

In the Amarna Period, when King Akhnaten revolutionized the religious and artistic life of the entire country, the king had himself represented in very private situations with his family in a way which no other king before him had done. The king has Nefertiti and some of his daughters on his lap; or Nefertiti tickles the king under his chin; or she embraces him while she ties a floral collar around his neck. Recently, a relief has been discovered showing the royal couple arm in arm in front of a bed. These scenes are most certainly not to be interpreted as overt exhibitionism on the part of the king, but as a ritualistic scene. It cannot be denied, however, that art in this particular period is more sensuous than ever before or after in Egypt.

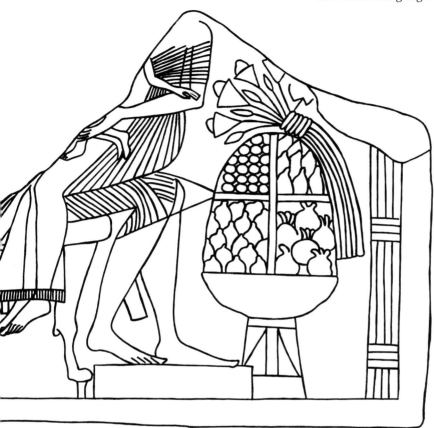

23. *Relief from el-Amarna, Louvre, Paris E. 11624.*

24. *Relief from el-Amarna, Ägyptisches*
    Museum, East Berlin 14511. 18th dyn.

The reticence of the Egyptians in displaying openly their intimate life does not mean that the representations lack in erotic tension. The erotic element is expressed in a symbolic way. In tombs belonging to high officials the walls are decorated with paintings and reliefs showing a number of activities. Apart from pictures of the gods, the funeral procession and the ceremonies connected with the burial, the so-called scenes of daily life depict the tomb owner in his office, fishing and fowling, supervising work in the fields, or dining with women at a banquet. The main purpose of having a tomb cut and decorated was to ensure eternal life in the Hereafter. The most important element to enable the deceased to go on existing was a constant

25. *Plaque from el-Amarna(?), Fitzwilliam Museum, Cambridge 4606.1943. 18th dyn.*

26. *Statuette from el-Amarna, University College London 002. 18th dyn.*

supply of food, combined with the rites that would make it possible for him to enjoy it. Heaps of offerings on the tables became real simply by being represented in the tomb; offering itemized lists served the same purpose. Depictions of work in fields equalled a never-ending supply of grain for bread and beer. It was the simplest of concepts expressed in a language understood by everyone. Other more sophisticated ideas on rebirth in the Hereafter were expressed in a code language also based on daily life, and so also was the sexual act which made rebirth possible in the first place.

Scenes showing the tomb owner fishing and fowling in the marshes along the banks of the river was not only a picture commemorating

27. *Relief in the tomb of Mereruka, Saqqara. 6th dyn.*

happy days of leisure. The tomb owner and his wife and children are shown on board a fragile canoe wearing their most festive outfits. The tomb owner always has a lucky day, harpooning two fish at a time, never just one. The key to the interpretation of the scene lies in these two fish, the *tilapia nilotica* which, to the Egyptians, was the very manifestation of the idea of rebirth. They had noticed that, in moments of danger, the *tilapia* was able to take its young in its mouth and spit it out again unharmed: apparently first killed, then re-born. On board the canoe, or in the hand of one of the women, sits a duckling or a goose. This bird had an erotic significance, perhaps it was even a symbol of female sexuality. Fowling with a throwstick also had a symbolic significance, though not particularly erotic in spite of the shape of the weapon. Fowling was one of the activities which Osiris, king of the dead, was able to resume, along with eating and speaking, after his death. By depicting this activity in the tomb, the tomb owner had taken steps to ensure that the same would happen to him in due course.

Banquet scenes appear to render an ideal feast with the tomb owner and his wife as the main characters, but they are so pregnant with

28. *Wall-painting in the tomb of Inherkhau (No. 359) at Deir el-Medina. 20th dyn.*

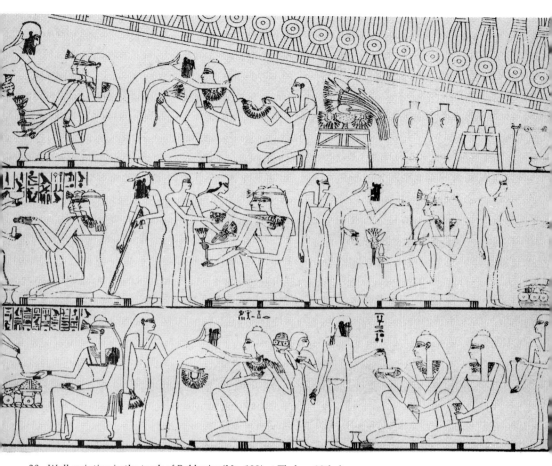

29. *Wall-painting in the tomb of Rekhmire (No. 100) at Thebes. 18th dyn.*

symbols, all pointing in the same direction, that there can be no doubt about the deeper significance of the occasion. Men and women sit in rows, the host and hostess usually seated apart from the rest of the party. Servants pour beer and wine, but no one ever eats anything. The guests receive necklaces made of lotus flowers and big lumps of solid unguent are placed on top of their wigs; during the course of the evening the fat melted and gave out a delightful scent of flowers and spices. The ladies wear diaphanous garments so thin that the breasts are visible through the linen, the curves of the legs and hips being emphasized by the fabric. They wear heavy and elaborately curled wigs, with plaits arranged according to the fashion of the day. They hold lotus flowers or lotus buds and mandrake fruits.

41

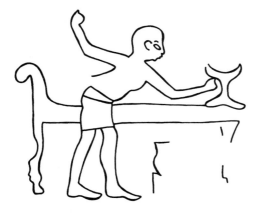

30. *Sketch on the wall of the tomb of Neferronpet (No. 140) at Thebes. 18th dyn.*

In Egypt the lotus flower was as significant as the flower of the pomegranate to the Greeks and red roses to us. The mandrake fruit was a symbol of love, the root being used in aphrodisiacs. Anything to do with hair has an erotic significance in all civilizations. So also in ancient Egypt. In one story the young man is even reported to have said: 'Don your wig and let us go to bed!'

The unguent cones underline the importance of scent in the erotic imagination of the Egyptians. They also much appreciated play on words; depicting servant girls pouring drinks to the guests must have reminded those with a mind so inclined of a sexual act, as both 'pouring' and 'ejaculating' were expressed by a similar sounding word, *seti*. (This word also meant 'to shoot' and, if the circumstances suggest it, scenes of hunting involving shooting may also have an underlying erotic significance.)

Thus the banquet scenes and the details consistently rendered point to a specific interpretation of the scenes as attempting to convey the initial stages in the rebirth proceedings in a language understood by those who knew the key to it. It is only during the past decade or so that this aspect of simple and idyllic scenes of the daily life of the ancient Egyptians has dawned on some scholars. The acceptance is by no means universal.

As mentioned above, the Egyptians did not consider that depicting certain parts of the body was unseemly, nor did they refrain from representing animals coupling. It has, presumably, nothing to do with seemliness if they did not choose to decorate their tombs with scenes of coupling human beings. Rather this was rooted in a firm belief that the magic force immanent in any picture might get out of control and, wherever anything sexual was concerned, it might be terrifying and harmful.

In the banquet scenes a little monkey (vervet) is often depicted under the chair of the tomb owner's wife. This might, of course, be a pet monkey, but with nothing in the scenes left to chance or for pure decoration, the presence of this animal must have an additional meaning. The explanation is obvious, for the monkey occurs in different contexts, most of which have a direct or indirect erotic

31. *Relief from the tomb of Queen Nefru at Deir el-Bahari, The Brooklyn Museum, New York acc. n. 54.49.*

43

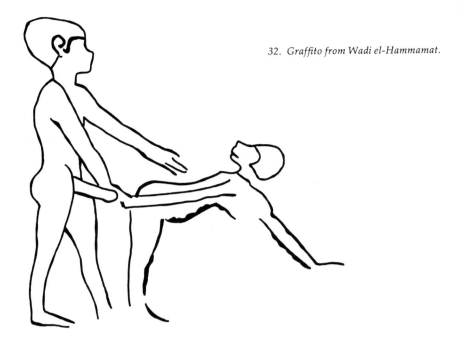

implication: some graffiti showing intercourse depict the female partner as having distinctly monkey-like features; cosmetic jars may be decorated with monkeys (one jar shows a woman in the same situation); monkeys with musical instruments are very likely to imitate female musicians; and one of the wives of Akhnaten had a name conspicuously similar to one of the words for monkey, and so did one of the ladies in his father's harem. Monkeys were evidently closely related to female sexuality, probably on a less subtle level than the duck or goose. The baboon which, in some instances, alternates with the monkey, had the phonetic value *nfr*, a word which cannot always be translated by one equivalent English word. 'Good', 'beautiful' and the like is the conventional rendering, but the word also implies something dynamic, creative and potent. When one symbol is replaced by another, they are often related, and it is interesting in this context that the monkeys may alternate with the dwarf god Bes, the protective god of the intimate life of women.

The Instruments of Love

Considering the attitude of the Egyptians to the magic power of any picture, it is no wonder that certain objects played a part in erotic situations. Amulettes and figurines were used in magic to obtain the love of a woman or to keep virility in the Hereafter. Hathor, the

33. *Part of a bed of ebony, Fitzwilliam Museum, Cambridge E.67c.1937. 18th dyn.*

goddess of music and love, was mistress of sistrum and *menat*, and these two objects were related to her special field. A sistrum is a sacred rattle, a *menat* was the counterpoise of a necklace, not in itself a musical instrument but used as such in that the counterpoise was used as a handle and the beads shaken. Both objects were used in temple rites, but also among mere mortals. The tomb owner and his wife are often being presented with them to wish the couple everlasting happiness and fertility.

34. *Ostrakon in a private collection.*

35. *Wall-painting from a Theban tomb, British Museum 37984. 18th dyn.*

The erotic rattling sound was reproduced by dancing girls at the banquet. They wore nothing but a string round their hips with hollow beads containing a little stone, giving out a seductive sound whenever the girls swayed their hips.

The Egyptian women used cosmetic appliances to make them even more attractive than nature had created them. Black eyepaint underlined their dark eyes, while lipstick and rouge added colour to the face. The cosmetic jars they used are decorated with erotic symbols as, for example, an unguent spoon shaped like the hieroglyph for life ⚲, the handle of which is adorned with a girl playing the lute while sailing along in a papyrus thicket. Both the lute and the boat are decorated with ducks' heads. Little jars for eyepaint made of anhydrite ('blue marble') have monkeys crawling round on the outside. Another unguent spoon is shaped like a swimming girl holding a duck, the hollow body of which contained the unguent. A faience bowl unites most of the erotic symbols in its decoration: a beautiful lute player squatting on a cushion while a monkey toys with her hip belt. She has the Bes tattoo of her profession on her thigh and wears an unguent cone and a lotus flower on her heavy wig. More flowers dangle from her elbows. The lute is decorated with a duck's head.

It is likely that the Egyptians employed a number of gadgets to enhance the physical aspect of erotic play, quite apart from the symbolic objects which were there to suggest discreetly what one had in mind.

36. *Unguent spoon from Sedment, University College London 14365. New Kingdom.*

37. *Decoration on a fayence bowl, Museum van Oudheden, Leiden AD 14/H 118/E.xlii.3 New Kingdom.*

38. Limestone figure from Saqqara.

In other ancient civilizations artificial phalloi were in use. But, although the Egyptians manufactured similarly shaped objects, there is nothing to indicate that they were ever used for anything but votive gifts. On the other hand, the erotic 'cartoon' reproduced towards the end of this book suggests that someone had thought of artificial stimulus. The girl who is painting her lips has positioned herself on top of an inverted vase with a pointed base. Her partner points his finger at her private parts. There can hardly be any doubt as to the purpose of this arrangement.

Musical instruments can often be seen in erotic contexts, particularly in Graeco-Roman figurines where the man's phallus is either

39. Wooden votive phallos from Deir el-Bahari.

40. *Fayence figurine, British Museum M39.*

41. *Wooden figurine, British Museum 48658. 19th dyn.*

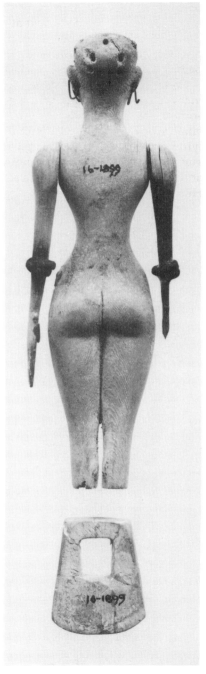

part of the musical instrument or is used for playing it. In pharaonic times orchestras are *de rigueur* at the banquets, the underlying significance of which has been discussed above. Lute and lyre are also present in the most intimate situations. Love and music always belonged together.

Concubine figurines were an important item in funerary equipment. They are dolls made of wood, faience and, occasionally, ebony, sometimes without feet but with the essential parts of the female anatomy underlined with paint or tattoos. Some of them are shown lying on a bed. Through magic they came alive in the tomb, excited and strengthened the virility of the tomb owner, gave him pleasure and, even more important, assured him miraculous rebirth in the Hereafter.

42. Ivory figurine, Fitzwilliam Museum E. 16.1899.

Erotic Texts

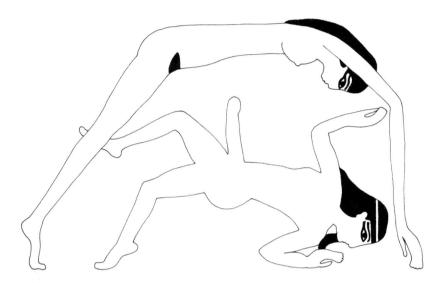

43. *Papyrus British Museum 10,008. 21st dyn.*

Mythological Tales

The creation of the world was instigated by the sun-god creating himself in the beginning. When this first step had been completed he produced two other gods, Shu, the air, and Tefenet, humidity, by masturbation. These two in turn united to create Geb, the earth, and Nut, the sky. Nut arched her back over Geb and, in the most obvious fashion, they became the parents of Osiris, Isis, Seth and Nephthys. With the later addition of Horus, son of Isis and Osiris, nine gods had now been created in the world: the Ennead. Other gods arrived and the scene was set for the play of which the very human characteristics of the gods were the origin.

A main theme was the contest of Horus and Seth as to which one of them was to take office after the death of Osiris: Horus, his son, or Seth, his brother – a most intricate legal problem. Both attempt to get the upper hand by more or less legitimate means, but in between the fights Seth finds time for adventure. Isis, in particular, was the object of his pursuits, but she rejects him. The following excerpt is to be found in various papyri (P. Chester Beatty I (*c.* 1600 BC)[17]; P. Kahun VI (*c.* 1900 BC)[18]; P. Jumilhac III (Ist cent. BC)[19].)

Episodes from life in the Ennead

The sun-god spent a great deal of his life taking sides and judging between the contestants. Once in a while, however, he did have the time to relax.

> The great god passed a day lying on his back in his arbour, and his heart was very sad, and he was alone.
> After a long time Hathor, lady of the southern sycamore, came and stood before her father, the master of the universe. She uncovered her vulva for his face, and the great god smiled at her. . . . (P. Chester Beatty I, 3, 13–4, 3)[20]

In the meantime Seth was trying for a spare moment with Isis.

> Seth looked and he saw her as she approached in the distance. Thereupon she uttered a magic spell, and she changed herself into a maiden fair of limbs, and there was not the like of her in the entire land, and he loved

44. *Limestone(?) figurine, British Museum.*

her very much. Thereupon he rose, and he went over to sit down and ate bread with the great Ennead. He went to overtake her, and no one had seen her except him.

Thereupon she stood behind a tree, and he shouted to her saying, 'I am here with you, fair maiden!' And she said to him, 'My great lord! As for me, I was the wife of a herdsman of cattle, and I bore him a male child. My husband died, and the boy came to watch the cattle of his father. But one day a stranger came and sat down in the stables and said to my son, "I'll beat you up and take your cattle and kick you out!" So he said. My greatest wish is for you to conquer him.'

Seth replied, 'Is the cattle to be given to a stranger when the son of the father is yet alive?'

At that moment Isis transformed herself into a kite and fled to the top of a tree. From there she shouted to Seth, 'Weep yourself. Your own mouth has said it, your own cleverness has given judgment. What more do you want?' (P. Chester Beatty I, 6, 3–7, 1)[21]

Isis refers to the situation concerning the legitimacy of inheriting the throne of Osiris, and she has obviously planned the entire set-up with this in mind, using her sex to trap Seth.

On another occasion it was Seth who exerted his power of transformation.

When Seth saw Isis there he transformed himself into a bull to be able to pursue her, but she made herself irrecognizable taking the appearance of a bitch with a knife on her tail. Then she began to run away from him, and Seth was unable to catch up with her. Then he ejaculated on the ground, and she said, 'It is disgusting to have ejaculated, you bull!' But his sperm grew in the desert and became the plants called *bedded-kau* (water melons?) (P. Jumilhac III, 1–6)[22]

Anat was a foreign goddess, a kind of Amazon who was adopted by the Ennead and who called the sun-god 'father', yet was also his wife. Seth soon succumbed to her vigorous beauty:

The goddess Anat was disporting herself in the stream of Khap and bathing in the stream of Hemket. Now the sun-god had gone out for a walk, and [he saw Seth as he mounted?] on her back, leaping her as a ram leaps. . . . [Then some of the seed flew] to his forehead near his brows and eyes. He lay down on his bed in his house [being ill. Then] came the divine Anat, the victorious, a woman acting as a warrior, clad as men and girt as women to Re, her father. And he said to her, 'What is the matter with you, Anat the divine, you the victorious, woman acting as a warrior, clad as men and girt as women? I came home in the evening, and I know that you have come to free Seth from the seed. Is it not a childish punishment for someone who was the wife of the sun-god that Seth should copulate with her in fire and open her with a chisel?' (P. Chester Beatty VII, verso, I, 5–II, 3)[23]

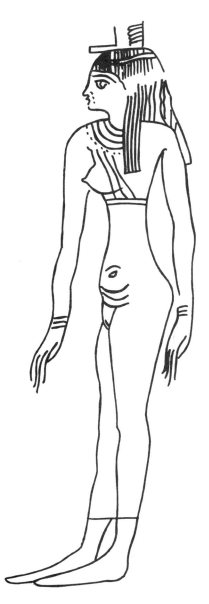

46. *Graffito in a tomb at Deir el-Bahari. New Kingdom.*

45. *Isis. Drawing on linen, Musée historique de Tissus, Lyon 55276 LA.*

47 and 48. *Ostraka in a private collection.*

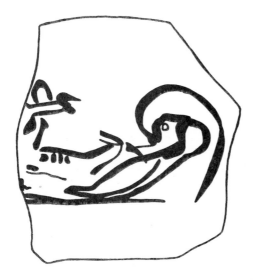

49. *Ostrakon from Deir el-Medina, Cairo IFAO 3962. New Kingdom.*

At some point the sun-god has enough of the contests of Horus and Seth, and he simply asks them to go away. Seth is in no doubt as to how they are to spend their time together.

Seth said to Horus, 'Come, let us spend a happy hour at my place!' Horus answered, 'Yes, with pleasure, with pleasure.' When it was evening the bed was spread for them and they lay down. During the night Seth made his member stiff, and he made it go between the loins of Horus. Horus put his hands between his loins, and he caught the seed of Seth.

Then Horus went to speak to his mother Isis, 'Come here, O Isis, my mother! Come and see what Seth has done to me!' And he opened his hand, and he showed her the seed of Seth. She cried out, seized her knife and cut off his hand, and she threw it into the water. But she took out another similar hand for him. Then she took a dab of sweet ointment and applied it to the member of Horus. She let it go stiff, having placed it in a jar, and she made his seed run into it.

50. *Graffito in a tomb at Deir el-Bahari. New Kingdom.*

In the morning she took the seed of Horus to Seth's garden. She said to his gardener, 'Which herb is it that Seth usually eats here with you?' The gardener replied, 'He does not eat any herb here except lettuce.' So Isis laid the seed of Horus on the lettuces.

Seth came as he used to do every day, and he ate the lettuces as usual. He became pregnant with the seed of Horus. He went and said to Horus, 'Come let us go that I can contend with you in the tribunal.' Horus said, 'I will do so, indeed, I will do so.'

Then they both went to the tribunal and stood before the great Ennead. They were told, 'Speak concerning yourselves!' Seth said, 'Let me be given the office of ruler, for as to Horus, the same that stands here, I have performed an aggressive act against him.'

The Ennead cried out aloud, and they belched and spat in the face of Horus. But Horus laughed at them, swore and said, 'All that Seth has said is false. Let the seed of Seth be summoned that we may see from where it will answer.'

Then Thoth, lord of divine words, the scribe of truth of the Ennead, placed his hand on the arm of Horus, and he said, 'Come out, you seed of Seth!' And it answered him from the water in the fen. Then Thoth placed his hand on the arm of Seth, and he said, 'Come out, you seed of Horus!' And it said to him, 'Where shall I come out?' Thoth said, 'Come out of his ear!' and it said, 'I who am divine effluence, shall I come out of his ear?' Then Thoth said, 'Come out of his forehead!'

And it came out as a golden disc on the head of Seth. Seth became extremely angry, and he reached out to lay hand on the golden disc. But Thoth took it away from him, and he placed it as an ornament on his own head. Then he said, 'Horus is in the right, and Seth is in the wrong.' Seth swore an oath and said, 'He shall not be given the office until we have sorted it out outside.' (P. Chester Beatty I, 11, 2–13, 3)[24]

Horus and Seth continue their strife by means of new tricks. In the end the problem is solved by despatching a letter to Osiris in the kingdom of the dead to let him give the final verdict. Horus becomes the successor to the throne.

There is a variant to the scene where Seth tries to rape Horus. It was clearly meant as a game of aggression, but Seth would not have been blind to the pleasure that went with it.

Seth said to Horus, 'How beautiful are your buttocks!' Horus replied, 'Wait that I may tell it [lacuna]'. . . . Horus said to his mother Isis, 'Seth wants to know me.' She said to him, 'Take care. Do not go near him for that. Next time he mentions it to you, you shall say to him, "It is too difficult for me because of my build, as you are heavier than I am. My strength is not the same as yours," you shall say to him. Then, when he has aroused you, you shall place your fingers between your buttocks. He will find it highly pleasant. . . . This seed which has come out of his phallus, the sun must not see it.' (P. Kahun VI, 2 recto)[25]

51. *Relief in the temple of Sethos I at Abydos. 19th dyn.*

How Isis conceived Horus

There are various explanations as to how Horus was created. According to one theological school he was created by the sun-god as part of the Ennead, but another tradition has it that he was conceived by Isis when Osiris, his father, was already dead. How this was possible is suggested by pictures of Osiris in the shape of a mummy lying on a couch, and Isis hovering above as a bird. With this picture in mind it is not difficult to interpret the texts which describe the act. A stela in the Louvre from about 1400 BC contains a hymn with the following passage:

Oh benevolent Isis,
who protected her brother Osiris,
who searched for him without wearying,
who traversed the land in mourning
and never rested until she had found him.
She who afforded him shadow with her wings
and gave him air with her feathers,
who rejoiced and carried her brother home.

58

52. *Stela, British Museum 1372. 13th dyn.*

> She who revived what was faint for the weary one,
> who received his seed and conceived an heir,
> and who nourished him in solitude
> while no one knew where he was. . . . (C286, 1. 15–6)[26]

Almost a thousand years later the same situation was described in different words (P. Louvre 3079, col. 110, 10)[27]:

> I am your sister Isis. There is no other god or goddess who has done what I have done. I played the part of a man, although I am a woman, to let your name live on earth, for your divine seed was in my body.

The divine conception of Queen Hatshepsut

It was essential for an Egyptian king to be able to prove that he had a legitimate right to the throne. If there was any doubt whatsoever, it was necessary to advertise a proclamation as to how the circumstances were quite special. Either it was said that the god had revealed himself to the young prince in a dream, or the statue of the god had pointed him out in the temple. Or perhaps the god himself was the father of the child. Queen Hatshepsut who ruled over Egypt as a king from 1503–1482 BC adopted this latter explanation. It was copied almost literally, later in the century, by King Amenophis III. The text is engraved on one of the walls of the queen's temple at Deir el-Bahari in Upper Egypt. The god Amun proclaims to the Ennead that he intends to engender a new ruler of Egypt. Thoth, the scribe, informs him that a beautiful queen, Ahmosis, lives in the royal palace. Amun is immediately interested, but he has a problem: how is he to get access to the queen's bedchamber to carry out his intent? The solution is delightfully simple: the god disguises himself as Tuthmosis I, husband of Queen Ahmosis.

> Amun found the queen in the inner rooms of the palace. When smelling the divine scent, she woke up, and she smiled to him. At once he proceeded towards her. He lusted after her, and he gave her his heart. He allowed her to see him in his real god's figure, having come close to her. She

59

rejoiced at his virility, and love for him flowed through her body. The palace became inundated by the scent of god, it smelled like in Punt (land of incense).

Thereupon the god did what he wished with her. She made him rejoice over her, and she kissed him. She said to him, 'How splendid it is to see you face to face. Your divine strength engulfs me, your dew is all through my limbs!' The god once more did what he wished with her, and he said, 'Truly, Hatshepsut will be the name of the child I have placed in your belly, for this was what you exclaimed.' (Urk. IV, 219, 13–220, 6)[28]

'Hatshepsut' may be translated 'the noble best' or the like, a worthy description of the god's performance.

Tales of Men

Egyptian erotic tales often mention adultery when the woman takes the initiative. In the end she fares badly. In real life as well adultery was a serious crime. According to Diodorus (I. 78, 3–4):[29]

If a man had violated a free married woman, they stipulated that he be emasculated. . . . If a man committed adultery with the woman's consent, the laws ordered that the man should receive a thousand blows with the rod, and that the woman should have her nose cut off. . . .

Administrative documents reveal how adultery flourished in the lower classes. A case from the Ramessid period tells how

Paneb raped the citizeness Tuy, when she was wife of the workman Kenna. He raped the citizeness Hunro, when she was living with Pendua. He raped the citizeness Hunro when she lived with Hesysunebef. So said his son. And after he had raped Hunro, he raped Webkhet, her daughter, and Apahte, his son, also raped Webkhet.

The document does not mention which punishment these illicit relationships merited.

A married woman who was discovered to have committed adultery was liable to be repudiated by her husband. A marriage contract of Ptolemaic date runs as follows: 'If I find you with any man in the world, I shall not be able to say to you any more, "You are my wife." ' But the woman had the possibility of swearing her innocence, saying, 'I did not have any extramarital intercourse. I have had no intercourse with anybody since I was married to you. . . .'

Webaoner's wife and the townsman

This tale is written on a scroll of papyrus, called Papyrus Westcar, now in East Berlin. It dates from about 1500 BC. The events take place

53. Ostrakon, British Museum 50,714. New Kingdom.

some thousand years prior to this date, being told at the court of King Cheops.

Webaoner (chief lector priest in the temple of Ptah at Memphis) had a wife who was in love with a townsman, and who kept in touch with him through a servant. She sent him a box full of clothes as a present, and one day he came with the servant girl.

Now there was a pleasure house in the lake of Webaoner, and after many days had passed the townsman said to the wife of Webaoner, 'Listen, there is a pleasure house in the lake of Webaoner. Come and let us spend some time there.'

The wife of Webaoner sent to the steward in charge of the lake, saying, 'Let the pleasure house in the lake be furnished.' Then she went there and spent the day drinking with the townsman until the sun set. When dusk had fallen, he went down into the lake, and the servant helped him bathing. The steward was watching them.

Now the following morning the steward went and reported the incident to his master. 'Fetch me my [instrument?] of ebony and gold,' said Webaoner, and with this he fashioned a waxen crocodile that was seven spans long. He recited a spell over it, and he said, 'Whosoever comes to bathe in my lake, seize him!' And he gave it to the steward and said to him, 'When the townsman goes down into the lake as he used to do every day, throw the crocodile into the water after him.' The steward went away and took the waxen crocodile with him.

61

Later Webaoner's wife sent for the steward in charge of the lake, saying, 'Let the pleasure house in the lake be furnished, for I want to go there.' And the pleasure house was furnished with all manner of good things. Then she went and spent a happy day with the townsman.

When dusk had fallen the townsman came as he used to do every day and went into the lake. The steward threw the waxen crocodile into the lake after him. It became a crocodile of seven cubits, and it seized the townsman. . . .

Webaoner stayed for seven days [in the temple of Ptah] with King Nebka, and in the meantime the townsman was in the water without breathing. When the seven days had passed . . . Webaoner said to King Nebka, 'May your Majesty come and view the wonder that has come to pass in the days of your Majesty.' The king went with him, and Webaoner called the crocodile and said, 'Bring up the townsman!' The crocodile came forth and brought him. 'What a terrifying crocodile!' exclaimed King Nebka. But Webaoner stepped down and took it, and it became a waxen crocodile in his hand.

Then the chief lector priest Webaoner related to the king this thing that the townsman had done in his house with his wife. And his Majesty said to the crocodile, 'Take what is yours!' Then the crocodile disappeared in the depths of the water [with the townsman], and no one knew where he went with him.

King Nebka let the wife of Webaoner be taken to the field to the north of the palace, and he set fire to her, and her ashes were thrown into the river.[30]

Bata and his sister-in-law

The tale of the wife of a man called Anubis and her attempt to seduce Bata, his little brother, is one of two stories which were joined together in ancient times and which are now known as 'The Story of the Two Brothers'. The manuscript, kept in the British Museum (P. d'Orbiney, BM 10, 183) was written down in the reign of Sethos II (*c.* 1210 BC).[31] The episode has an obvious parallel in the biblical tale of the wife of Potiphar.

There once were two brothers of the same mother and father. Anubis was the name of the elder, Bata the name of the younger. Anubis had a house and a wife, and his younger brother lived with him in the manner of a son. He made clothes for him and took his cattle to the field. He ploughed the fields, and he harvested the grain. He looked after everything in the field. Yes, the younger brother was a vigorous young man, there was not his like in the entire country. There was the strength of a god in him.

Some time after this Bata was watching the cattle as he used to do. Every evening he came home loaded with all kinds of herbs from the field, milk and wood and all good things from the field. He laid it before Anubis who was sitting with his wife. Then he ate and drank, and he went to sleep with the animals in the stables. When the day grew light, he made breakfast and served it to his elder brother. Anubis gave him provisions to bring to the field. While Bata watched the cattle, the cows said to him, 'The grass is nice over there.' Bata heard all that they said, and he took them to the place with the grass they liked. The cows he looked after grew exceedingly beautiful, and they doubled their calves.

One day during sowing time Anubis said to Bata, 'Yoke a span of oxen, for the soil has emerged from the inundation, and it is good for ploughing. And come back with the seed, for we must be ready for ploughing early in the morning.' So he said, and Bata did all that his elder brother told him.

The following day they took the seed to the field, and they started ploughing. They were exceedingly satisfied with their work from the beginning. One of the following days, while they were in the field and ran out of seed, Anubis sent to his brother saying, 'Go and fetch us seed from the village.'

Bata found the wife of his elder brother as she sat doing her hair. He said to her, 'Get up and give me seed that I may go to the field, for my elder brother is waiting for me. Do not tarry.' She said to him, 'Go, open the bin yourself and take what you like, so that I shall not have to leave my wig on the ground.'

Bata went to the stable and took a great vessel, for he intended to take a lot of seed. He loaded himself with barley and wheat and carried it outside on his shoulders. She said to him, 'How much is it that you have upon your shoulder?' 'Three sacks of wheat and two sacks of barley,' he replied. 'Five in all I have upon my shoulder.' 'You are very strong,' she said. 'Every day I see how strong you are.' And she desired to know him as one knows a man. She arose and took hold of him and said, 'Come, let us spend an hour together! It will be to your advantage, for I shall make you a nice dress.'

But Bata became enraged like a panther because of her wicked proposal, and she became afraid. He said to her, 'Look, you are to me as a mother, and your husband is to me as a father, for he is my elder brother, he has

54. *Ostrakon from Deir el-Medina in private collection. New Kingdom.*

63

brought me up. What is this abominable thing you have just said? Do not say it to me again. I will tell it to no one, I will not let it cross my lips to anyone.' Bata took his load and went into the field. He came to his brother, and they continued their work.

In the evening Anubis went home, but Bata stayed behind watching the cattle. He loaded himself with all manner of things from the field, and he drew his cattle before him to let them sleep in the village.

But the wife of Anubis was afraid because of what she had said. She took fat and a rag(?) and made herself up as though she had been beaten, with the intention of saying to her husband, 'Your younger brother has beaten me up.'

When Anubis came home as usual and arrived at the house, he found his wife lying down pretending to be sick. She did not pour water over his hands as he was used to. She had lit no lamp for him, and the house was in darkness. There she lay and vomited. 'Who has talked to you?' her husband inquired. She replied, 'No one has talked to me except your younger brother. When he came to fetch the seed and found me sitting all alone, he said to me, "Come, let us sleep together for an hour! Don your wig!" So he said to me. But I refused to listen to him. "Look, am I not like your mother, and is your elder brother not like your father?" I said to him. Then he became frightened. He beat me so that I may not tell you. Therefore, if you allow him to live, I shall die. And by the way, when he comes home tonight, do not listen to him, for it makes me sick to think of the wicked proposal he intended to carry through.'

Anubis became enraged like a panther. He sharpened his lance and took it in his hand. He positioned himself behind the door of the stables in order to kill his brother when he came home to let the cattle in. When the sun set, Bata loaded all sorts of herbs on his shoulders as he used to do and set out for home. When the head cow entered the stables she said to her herdsman, 'Look, your elder brother is there in front of you with his lance to kill you. Run away from him.' Bata heard what the cow said. The next cow entering said the same. Then he looked underneath the door of the stables, and he saw the feet of his elder brother as he stood there with the lance in his hand. Bata laid down his load and began running. Anubis followed him lance in hand.

Then Bata invoked Re-Harakhte saying, 'My good lord! You are the one who tells the truthful one from the liar.' The god heard his prayer, and he created a lake full of crocodiles between Bata and his elder brother. They stood there on either side of the lake. Anubis hit his hand twice because he had not succeeded in killing his brother. Bata shouted from the other bank of the lake, 'Stay here until tomorrow morning. When the sun rises I shall be judged in front of it, and it will deliver the liar to the truthful one. I will never be with you any more. I shall go to the Pine Valley.'

When the day came Re arose. Bata and Anubis stood there looking at each other. Bata said to his elder brother, 'Why is it that you run after me to kill me because of a lie and without having heard what I have to say? I am indeed your younger brother, and you have been as a father to me.

Your wife was like a mother to me. When you sent me to fetch us seed, your wife said to me, "Come, let us sleep together for an hour!" But look how she twisted it into something else for you.' And he reported all that had happened between him and his sister-in-law. Then he swore an oath by Re-Harakhte saying, 'Imagine that you should want to slay me because of a lie, lance in hand, instigated by a vulva of a whore.' Thereupon he took a sharp reed and cut off his member and threw it into the water where the shad swallowed it.

Bata became weak and miserable. His elder brother grew sick at heart, and he stood there weeping loudly without being able to cross the lake to the other side where his brother was because of the crocodiles. Bata shouted at him, 'You only thought of wicked things, not of the good, nor of any of the things I have done for you. Go home and look after your cattle yourself, for I will no longer be where you are. I shall go to the Pine Valley.'

Anubis returned home, and he killed his wife, and he threw her to the dogs. Then he sat down and wept over his younger brother.

Bata did indeed go to the Pine Valley where a dramatic series of events took their beginning. But this is another story. . . .

Erotic amulet, British Museum.

Setne and Tabubu

A man who had intercourse with a woman other than his legal wife might find himself in trouble. Setne, for instance, would have fared better if he had heeded the advice of Ptahhotpe, the sage:

> If you want to maintain friendship in the house wherever you go as a master, as brother or as friend, beware of approaching the women. It is not good to be where such things are done. It needs little cunning to divide them. A thousand men may be led astray for what is good for them. A brief moment, like a dream, and you are close to death through knowing them.

Setne's passion for the beautiful Tabubu very nearly had disastrous results. The tale is written on Papyrus Cairo 30646,[32] copied during the Ptolemaic period sometime in the first century BC. Setne was one of the many sons of Ramesses II who had ruled over Egypt some thousand years earlier. He was a priest and had acquired the reputation of being a magician. It was indeed his interest in magic that was the cause of his affair with Tabubu. A colleague of his, called Neneferkaptah, had acquired under the most trying circumstances a book of magic written by Thoth, the god of magic himself. Setne desired to possess it; to begin with he tries to steal it and bully Neneferkaptah into handing it over. Neneferkaptah suggests a more dignified solution: Setne must try and win the book from him over a board game. Being a magician makes winning easy, but both of them are equally ingenious. In the end Setne manages to get hold of the book. He cannot refrain from boasting of the fact. He even tells Pharaoh who advises him to hand it back. Setne refuses to listen; he continues to go around and read aloud from the book. . . .

> It happened one day that Setne was walking around in the forecourt of the temple of Ptah. Then he caught sight of a very beautiful woman. There was not a woman like her in appearance. She was beautiful and wore many golden jewels. There were maid servants walking behind her as well as two man servants from her household. The moment Setne saw her he lost count of where he was. He called his valet, saying, 'Hurry to the place where this woman is, and find out what her situation is.' The valet hurried to the place where the woman was. He called to the maid who was following

55. *Drawing on wood from a Theban tomb (now lost). New Kingdom.*

her and asked her, 'What woman is this?' She told him, 'It is Tabubu, daughter of the priest of Bastet, mistress of Ankhtawy. She has come here to worship Ptah, the great god.'

The valet returned to Setne and told him every word she had said to him. Setne said to him, 'Go and say to the maid, "It is Setne Khaemwas, son of Pharaoh Usermare, who has sent me to say, 'I will give you ten pieces of gold if you will sleep with me for an hour. Or do you have a complaint against someone? I'll have it settled for you. I will have you taken to a secret place where no one on earth shall find you." '

The valet returned to the place where Tabubu was. He called her maid and told her. She cried out as if what he had said was an insult. Tabubu said to the valet, 'Stop talking to this stupid maid. Come and talk to me.' The valet hurried to Tabubu and said to her, 'I will give you ten pieces of gold. Sleep for an hour with Setne Khaemwas, son of Pharaoh Usermare. If you have a complaint against someone he will have it settled for you. He will take you to a secret place where no one on earth shall find you.'

Tabubu said, 'Go, tell Setne this: "I am of priestly rank. I am not a low person. If you desire to do what you wish with me, you must come to my house in Bubastis. It is well furnished, and you shall do what you wish with me without anyone on earth finding me and without my behaving like a woman of the street." '

The valet returned to Setne and told him all that she had said to him. Setne said, 'That suits me fine!' Everyone around Setne was indignant.

Setne had a boat brought to him. He went on board and hurried to Bubastis. When he came to the west of the suburb he found a tall house with a wall around it, a garden to the north, and a bench near the door. 'Whose house is this?' asked Setne. 'It is the house of Tabubu,' they told him. Setne went inside the wall. As he was facing the storehouse in the garden they announced him to Tabubu. She came down, took Setne's hand and said to him, 'By the happiness of the house of the priest of Bastet, mistress of Ankhtawy to which you have come, it will please me greatly if you would oblige to come upstairs with me.'

Setne climbed the stairs of the house with Tabubu. He found the upper story of the house swept and decorated, its floor adorned with real lapis lazuli and real turquoise. There were many couches there, spread with the finest linen, and many golden cups were on the table. A golden cup was filled with wine and placed in Setne's hand. Tabubu said to him, 'Please eat something.' He said to her, 'I could not do that.' Incense was laid on the brazier, and ointment of the kind provided by Pharaoh was brought to him. Setne amused himself with Tabubu. He had never seen anyone like her before.

Setne said to Tabubu, 'Let us accomplish what we came here for.' But she replied, 'Return to your own house. I am of priestly rank. I am not a low person. If you desire to do what you wish with me you must make out a deed of maintenance for me and a deed of compensation in cash for everything that belongs to you.' Setne ordered, 'Send for the school teacher!' He was brought at once. He made out a deed of maintenance and compensation in cash for everything that belonged to him to her benefit.

At this moment they came to announce to Setne, 'Your children are downstairs.' He said, 'Let them be brought up!' Tabubu rose and put on a garment of the finest linen. Setne could see all her limbs through it, and he lusted after her even more than he had done before. He said, 'Tabubu, let me accomplish what I came here for!' But she replied, 'Return to your own house. I am of priestly rank. I am not a low person. If you desire to do what you wish with me, you must make your children subscribe to my deed. Do not leave them to haggle with my children over your property.' Setne had his children brought and made them subscribe to the deed. Then he said, 'Tabubu, let me accomplish what I have come for!' But she replied, 'Return to your own house. I am of priestly rank. I am not a low person. If you desire to do what you wish with me, you must have your children killed. Do not leave them to haggle with my children over your property.' Setne said, 'Let the disgusting idea you had be carried out!' And Tabubu had his children killed in front of him. She had them thrown from the windows to the dogs and cats. They ate their flesh, and Setne heard them as he sat drinking with Tabubu.

Then Setne said, 'Tabubu, let us accomplish what we came here for! I have done all the things you suggested.' She said, 'Come with me to the storehouse.' Setne went there. He lay down on a couch of ivory and ebony, his wish about to be fulfilled. Tabubu lay down beside him. He stretched out his hand to touch her, and she opened her mouth wide in a loud cry.

Setne awoke in a state of great heat. His phallus was erect, and he had no clothes on at all.

At this moment Setne saw a nobleman carried in a litter, with many men running beside him. The man looked like Pharaoh. Setne was about to get up, but he could not for shame, for he had no clothes on. Pharaoh said, 'Setne, what a state you are in!' Setne answered, 'It is Neneferkaptah who has caused all this!' Pharaoh said, 'Go to Memphis. Your children need you. They stand in their rank before Pharaoh.' Setne said to Pharaoh, 'My great lord – O may you have the lifetime of Re! – how can I go to Memphis with no clothes on at all?' Pharaoh sent for the servant who was standing near by and made him fetch clothes for Setne. Pharaoh said, 'Setne, go to Memphis. Your children are alive. They stand in their rank before Pharaoh.'

When Setne came to Memphis he embraced his children, for he found them alive. Pharaoh said to him, 'Were you drunk when I saw you earlier on?' Setne told him everything that had happened with Tabubu and Neneferkaptah. Pharaoh said, 'Setne, I told you so before: they will kill you if you do not take the book back to the place from which you took it. You have not listened to me until now. Take the book back to Neneferkaptah.'

And so Setne did.

The previous tales have been preserved almost in their entirety. But papyrus is a fragile material, and often fragments only have survived after millennia in the sand. Even the tiniest fragment, however, may open the door to a new literary genre, and with some imagination it is perhaps possible to envisage the beginning and the end of this scrap of an erotic tale.

The herdsman and the goddess

This story is found on Papyrus 3024 in Berlin, written around 1900–1800 BC.[33] The same scroll contains another well-known text, 'The Man who was Tired of Life'. Only twenty-five lines of text survive of the story of the herdsman who went to take his cows to the field but was met by an astonishing sight. We enter the story as he relates it to his mates.

> 'Lo and behold, when I went down to the swamp which borders on this low ground, I saw a woman there, and she looked not like an ordinary mortal. My hair stood on end when I saw her tresses, because her colour was so smooth. Never will I do what she suggested. I am terrified of her.' [The storyteller urges the herdsman to take his cattle home and perhaps to forget about it. But . . .] when the earth grew bright at early dawn, what he had said did happen. The goddess met him at the pool, and she had stripped off her clothes and disarrayed her hair. . . .

56. Wall-painting in the tomb of Neferhotep (No. 49) at Thebes. 18th dyn.

Truth and falsehood

From Papyrus 10682 in the British Museum,[34] written around 1300 BC, comes the following story. The main characters are neither gods nor men, but two abstract ideas, yet with very human feelings. Falsehood has lent a knife to his brother Truth and wants him to return it. Truth must have refused, for Falsehood takes him to court. The judges are the members of the great Ennead, whom we have met before. Falsehood suggests that Truth has his eyes put out and be made a door keeper, and the Ennead consents. As if that were not enough, Falsehood attempts to have him thrown to the lions. But Truth cunningly escapes and wanders about in the desert for several days. Then something unexpected happens.

> One of the following days a lady came out of her house with her servants. They saw Truth lying at the foot of the hill. He was handsome, as handsome as no one else in the entire country. The servants hurried to their mistress saying, 'Come and see the blind man lying at the foot of the hill. Let us bring him home and make him our door keeper!' Their mistress replied, 'Go and fetch him that I may see him.' They went to fetch him. And when the lady saw him, she desired him very, very much, for she had noticed how handsome he was all over.
>
> He slept with her that night, and he knew her as a man knows a woman. That night she conceived a little boy.

57. Ostrakon, Egyptian Museum, Cairo 11198. New Kingdom.

Many days after this she gave birth to a boy, whose like was not in the entire land and who looked like a young god. He was sent to school, and he learnt to write, and he excelled in sports and was the champion of the boys at the school who were his senior.

One day his schoolmates said to him, 'Whose son are you? Indeed, you have no father?' They mocked and teased him and said, 'Indeed you have no father!' Then the boy said to his mother, 'What is the name of my father that I may tell my schoolmates, for they tease me and say, "Where is your father?" So they say, and they nag me.' Then his mother answered, 'Do you see the blind man over there at the door? He is your father.' Thereupon he said to her, 'We must have a family council and fetch a crocodile [in order to seize you who have shamelessly slept with the door-keeper].' The boy went to get his father, and he sat him on a chair and put a stool under his feet. He gave him bread and let him eat and drink. Then he said to his father, 'Who blinded you that I may take revenge?' He said, 'My younger brother blinded me.' And he told him all that had happened, and the boy went to revenge his father.

The boy persuades the herdsman of Falsehood to watch a cow of his which is so magnificent that Falsehood steals it, replacing it with another cow. Now Falsehood is taken to court and he swears that he will have his eyes put out if only Truth is found alive. This takes place and, in addition, Falsehood receives one hundred strokes and is made doorkeeper in the house of Truth.

Pharaoh often appears in Egyptian tales, either as an unnamed king or under his real name. It has already been demonstrated how Pharaoh played a minor part in the stories of Webaoner's wife and Setne and Tabubu. But sometimes Pharaoh was the main character. King Seneferu, for example, appreciated the beauty of women. This poetic account is to be found in the same manuscript as that containing the story of Webaoner's wife. Both stories concern remarkable incidents which were told to King Cheops, the great pyramid builder.

King Seneferu and the twenty maidens

King Seneferu walked through every room of the palace looking for something with which to amuse himself. But he found nothing amusing. So he said, 'Go and fetch Djadja-em-ankh!'

The magician was brought to the king at once. The king said to him. 'I have walked through every room in the palace looking for something to amuse me, but I have found nothing.'

Djadja-em-ankh replied, 'I suggest that you go to the palace lake and order a boat and call for some young girls from your palace. Watching them row up and down will cheer you up.'

71

The king said, 'Yes, I shall arrange a boating party. Let twenty oars decorated with gold be brought to me. Let twenty women with beautiful limbs and breasts and braids, twenty young women who have not borne children. And twenty fish nets as well. Let the nets be draped on the women, when they have taken their clothes off.'

It was then done exactly as the king had commanded. The women rowed up and down, and the king was happy as he watched them rowing. But suddenly the girl who stood at the helm and steered the boat got something caught in her braid. It was her new turquoise amulet, and as she pulled it free, it dropped into the water. She stopped steering, and then all the women on her side of the boat stopped rowing.

The king said, 'Why are you stopping?'

They replied, 'Because our girl at the helm has stopped steering.'

So the king asked the helmsgirl, 'Why don't you go on steering the boat?'

And she replied, 'My amulet has fallen into the water.'

The king said, 'I shall give you another one just like it!'

But she answered, 'I want my own, not another one!'

Then the king said to his messenger, 'Go and fetch Djadja-em-ankh the magician.' He was brought to the king at once.

The king said, 'My dear Djadja-em-ankh. I have done as you suggested, and I was happy as I watched the girls row. Then a new turquoise amulet, which belonged to the girl at the helm, fell into the water, and she stopped steering the boat. I asked her, "Why don't you steer the boat?" and she answered, "My new turquoise amulet has fallen into the water." So I said to her, "Sail on, and I shall give you another one just like it." But she said, "I don't want another one, I want my own." '

Then Djadja-em-ankh uttered some magic words, and he folded one half of the water in the lake right over on top of the other. And there was the girl's amulet, lying on a broken pot at the bottom of the lake, where the water had been moved away. The magician picked up the amulet and returned it to its owner. But the water in the lake, which normally was 12 cubits deep, was now 24 cubits deep where it had been folded in the middle.

So once again Djadja-em-ankh uttered some magic words, and he put the water of the lake back the way it belonged again.

Thus the king had a delightful time after all, and so did everyone in the palace. And at the end of the day Djadja-em-ankh, the magician, was rewarded with fine gifts.

Now this was a miraculous event that happened in the days of King Seneferu.[35]

A quite different story was told of King Neferkare who lived about 350 years later than King Seneferu. This king is better known as Pepi II and, according to one tradition, he reigned no less than ninety-nine years, having ascended the throne at the age of six. No wonder that he felt in need of some variation in his private life, as suggested by the following tale, written on a papyrus now in the Louvre (E 25351)[36] during the 25th dynasty (around 700 BC). The beginning of the story also survives on a tablet dating to the New Kingdom (OIC 13539).

King Neferkare and his general

A man called Teti, son of Henut, sees his king go out all on his own in the night.

> His Majesty, the King of Upper and Lower Egypt Neferkare, went off at night all on his own, no one being with him. Teti moved away so as not to be seen by him. He stood still and said to himself, 'Things being what they are, it seems to be true what they say: he goes out by night.'
>
> Teti, son of Henut, followed at the heels of the king without any qualms in order to find out what he was up to. He arrived at the house of general Sisene. He threw a brick and kicked his foot on the ground, whereupon a ladder(?) was lowered to him. The king climbed up, while Teti stayed below to await his return. When his Majesty had completed doing what he wanted with the general, he returned to the palace, and Teti followed him. When the king had entered the palace, Teti went home.
>
> His Majesty had gone to the house of general Sisene when four hours of the night had passed, and he had spent another four hours there. And he only returned to the palace when four hours were left before dawn.

Figurine, British Museum.

*58. Ostrakon from Deir el-Medina,
Cairo IFAO 3062. New Kingdom.*

Love Poems

To the Egyptians the name of a thing or a person was of paramount importance. This had to do with the magic force innate in a word or picture. The hieroglyphic language consisted of pictures and, for this reason, words and pictures were firmly linked together. From the most ancient times the Egyptians used the magic of the word to ensure a safe life in the hereafter, or to be on favourable terms with the gods. Hymns, prayers and formulas were recited and, by sheer magic, they were able to alter reality. When during the New Kingdom (1580–1085 BC) love poems make their first appearance, they were easily fitted into an existing lyrical form. The poems are in prose, there are no rhymes, but there is a certain rhythm which may be difficult to enjoy in full nowadays when no one knows how the language was actually pronounced. The poems are loaded with symbolism and there is much play on words.

The language employed is simple and straightforward and by no means obscene. It is about love, not about copulation, and thus the poems are different from the coarser mythological tales. Not that the Egyptians were short of words in this respect: there were at least a dozen words to describe the act of 'intercourse'.

In the poems one or the other of the lovers speaks, or it is a third party, 'the poet', who lends his anonymous voice.

On the verso of the papyrus describing the contests of Horus and Seth (P. Chester Beatty I in Dublin) there is a collection of poems

74

which describes the happiness and despair of a person in love, written 3000 years ago. As in other poems the lovers address each other as 'sister' and 'brother', but this has absolutely nothing to do with incest.

There is a play of words between the number of the poem and one of the words in the first line, but this can only be rendered successfully in the translation of the first verse.

She is one girl, there is no one like her.
She is more beautiful than any other.
Look, she is like a star goddess arising
at the beginning of a happy new year;
brilliantly white, bright skinned;
with beautiful eyes for looking,
with sweet lips for speaking;
she has not one phrase too many.
With a long neck and white breast,
her hair of genuine lapis lazuli;
her arm more brilliant than gold;
her fingers like lotus flowers,
with heavy buttocks and girt waist.
Her thighs offer her beauty,
with a brisk step she treads on the ground.
She has captured my heart in her embrace.
She makes all men turn their necks
to look at her.
One looks at her passing by,
this one, the unique one.

My brother troubles my heart with his voice,
he makes me feel almost ill.
he is a neighbour of my mother's,
yet I cannot go to him.
My mother does well when she says to him,
'Stop seeing her!'
for look, my heart is anxious when I think of him,
for I have fallen in love with him.
Look, he has lost his senses,
but I – I am like him.
He knows not my desire to embrace him,
or he would send to my mother.
O brother, the golden goddess of women
has decreed me unto you.
Come to me that I may see your beauty.
My father and mother will be glad,
everybody will rejoice at you unanimously.
they will rejoice at you, o my brother.

59. Ostrakon from Deir el-Medina in private collection. New Kingdom.

My heart knew not to see its(?) beauty
while I sat in there.
But then I found Mehy riding on the road
with his young friends.
I knew not how to behave in front of him.
Should I pass him with swift steps?
Or should I escape by the river?
I know not where to put my feet.
How stupid you are, my heart,
why will you run away from Mehy?
Look, if I pass before him,
I shall tell him what is the matter.

'Look, I'm yours,' I shall say to him,
and he will boast of me,
and allot me to the best harim
of some one among his followers.

My heart flees quickly
when I think of my love for you.
It will not let me walk like a human,
it is scared from its place.
Because of it I cannot don a tunic,
nor can I wear my gown(?).
I cannot make my eyes up,
nor anoint myself at all.
'Do not stand there. Go home!'
it tells me whenever I think of him.
Pretend not to be a fool, my heart.
Why do you play the fool?
Sit quiet until the sister comes to you,
my eye is equally sullen(?).
Let not people say:
She is a woman crazy with love.
Stand fast as often as you think of him,
o my heart, do not flee!

I adore the golden goddess, I praise her majesty,
I exalt the lady of heaven,
I give praise to Hathor and thank my mistress.
I appealed to her, and she heard my appeal,
she sent to me my mistress,
and she herself came to see me.

60. *Hathor. Ostrakon from Deir
el-Medina, Louvre, Paris E. 12966.
New Kingdom.*

How great is that which has happened to me!
I rejoice, I exult, I feel important
ever since it was said, 'Look, here she is.'
Look, when she came, the young men bowed
for they love her so much.
I implore my goddess
that she give me the sister as a gift.
Three days it is to yesterday
since I first mentioned her in my prayers,
but she has not been here for five days.

I passed by his house,
I found his door open.
My brother was standing next to his mother,
and all his sisters and brothers.
All who passed by were enraptured by him,
a fine young man, without his like,
a man of excellent character.
He looked at me when I passed by,
and I was alone to rejoice.
How happy I am, o my brother
because you saw me.
If only my mother had known my heart
she would have gone in.
O golden goddess, let her understand,
and I will hurry to my brother.
I will kiss him before his friends.
I would not weep over anyone,
but I would rejoice that they realize
that you know me.

I will make a feast for my goddess.
My heart trembles and wants to flee.
It will make my brother look at me tonight.
How happy is the passing of the night!

61. *Ostrakon from Deir el-Medina,
Cairo IFAO 3971. New
Kingdom.*

Seven days it is from yesterday since I saw my sister,
and I am feeling all ill.
My limbs are heavy, I forget my body.
If the doctors come, no remedies will cure me,
even the lector priests know not the cure.
There is no diagnosis for my disease.
What I have said is what revives me.
Her name can get me on my feet.
The coming and going of her messengers
is what revives my heart.

More beneficial to me than any remedies is my sister.
More important is she to me than any medical book.
My salvation is her coming in.
When I see her, then I feel well!
When she opens her eyes, my limbs are young again.
When she speaks, then I am strong.
When I embrace her, she drives away all evil from me.
But she has been gone for seven days.
(P. Chester Beatty I, verso C1–C5, 2)

On the same scroll of papyrus there are three poems in which 'the poet' speaks, not the lovers themselves, encouraging the young man to hasten to his beloved.

O come to your sister quickly,
like a royal envoy
whose lord impatiently awaits his message,
for he is anxious to hear it.
For this envoy all stables have been commissioned,
he has horses at every resting place.
The chariot is harnessed in its place.
He cannot rest upon the road.
When he reaches the house of his beloved.
his heart rejoices.

O come to your sister quickly,
like a royal stallion,
picked from a thousand steeds of every kind,
the best one of the stables.
It has the best provender of all,
its lord knows its paces.
If it hears the sound of the whip,
nothing will restrain it.
Nor is there a charioteer
who can draw level with it.
The heart of the sister knows well
that he is not far away.

O come to your sister quickly,
like a gazelle bounding over the desert,
its feet are weary, its limbs are faint,
for a huntsman is chasing it,
and dogs are with him.
But they see not its dust,
for it has found a place to rest.
It has taken to the river.
You shall reach its grotto
before your hand is kissed four times.
You seek the sister's love.
The golden goddess has decreed her to you,
o my friend.
(P. Chester Beatty I, verso G1, 1–G2, 5)[37]

62. *Ostrakon from Deir el-Medina,
Cairo IFAO 3793. New
Kingdom.*

The young man in love is compared to a messenger storming forward.
He is like a stallion who cannot be held back and like a gazelle being
chased until it stumbles with fatigue. 'You shall reach its grotto,' it
says. Or perhaps 'her grotto', for in Egyptian the pronoun is the same
in both cases. The *double entendre* is quite deliberate. The grotto is a
discreet hint as to the pleasures awaiting the young man.

Papyrus Chester Beatty I also contains a number of poems copied
from a more ancient scroll. The title is as follows: 'The beginning of
the sweet verses found in a scroll case and written by Sobknakht of
the necropolis'.[38]

When you go to the house of the sister
and charge towards her grotto,
the gate is made high.
Its mistress cleans it
and furnishes it with the palate's delight,
exquisite wines, specially reserved.
You confound her senses(?)
but stops at night when she says to you,
'Hold me tight that we may lie like this
when dawn comes.'

*63. Design on a mirror case,
Egyptian Museum Cairo CG
44101. 21st dyn.*

When you go to the room of the sister,
she being alone and without another,
you can do what you wish with the latch.
The door hangings flutter
when the sky comes down in the wind,
but it does not carry it away,
that is, her fragrance
when she brings you an abundance of scent,
intoxicating those present.
It is the golden goddess who has sent her as a reward
until the end of your life.

How clever is the sister in casting the noose.
She is not the child of a cattle-breeder,
but casts the noose after me with her locks.
Having caught me with her eye
and fettered me with her buttocks,
she brands me with her seal.

When you say to your heart,
'After her! her embrace is mine!'
By Amun! It is I who come to you
with my gown over my arm.

I found the brother on the other side of the canal
with one leg in the water.
he spends the day having a drinking bout
with his beer companions.
He brings colour to my cheeks
by vomiting persistently.(?)

As for what the sister did to me
should I be silent for her sake?
That she left me to stand in the doorway,
while she herself went in.
She did not say 'Welcome',
but stayed aloof all night.

She who sang to me was Tashere of the music room of the children of the
mayor.
(P. Chester Beatty I, recto XVI, 9–XVII, 7)[39]

The postscript reveals that these verses were actually sung and, for once, we have the name of the performing artist. The songs would appear to be intended for the entertainment of visitors in private houses. Several *double entendres* can be read in and between the lines, but it remains an open question to what extent they were intended. Perhaps the ancient audience was left guessing, too.

The poetic setting of the garden inspired a number of love poems. A papyrus in Turin (No. 1966 recto)[40] includes a discussion among the fruit trees in the orchard as to which one serves their mistress best. It dates from the New Kingdom, around 1175 BC.

64. Wall-painting in the tomb of Neferhotep (No. 49) at Thebes. 18th dyn.

The pomegranate opens its mouth to say,
'My seeds are like her teeth, my fruits are like her breasts.
I am the foremost in the orchard, for I endure through every season.
The sister spends the day with the brother under my branches,
drunk with grape and pomegranate wine,
besprinkled with fragrance of resin.
All the other trees in the meadow perish, except I,
for I complete the twelve months. I remain.
If this flower drops, another will break through from within.
I am the foremost in this orchard,
yet they rate me second.
If they repeat it once more,
I shall no longer remain silent about them.
Look, when their misdeeds are revealed,
the lovers will be taught a lesson,
and she will not . . . her stalk of lotus flowers and buds.
He begins to feel the strong ale.
She lets him spend a merry day.
The reed hut is like a guardsman's house.
"Look, it is light," (said she). "Come,
let us flatter it. Let it spend the entire day.
After all, it is the pomegranate that lends us its hiding place." '

The fig tree moves its mouth, and its leaves begin to speak,
'How good it is to obey my mistress's orders.
She is a true lady.
If there are no servants,
I'll be the slave,
having been brought from the land of Kharu as a trophy of love.
She had me planted in her orchard.
But she does not allow me a drink
on the day of drinking.
She does not fill my belly with water from the water skin.
It seems that they are enjoying themselves and laughing,
yet I am deprived of drinking.
My soul! My beloved, may she be brought forward!'

The little sycamore fig which she planted with her own hand
moves its mouth to speak.
Its voice is like liquid honey. It is beautiful.
Its leaves are pretty, greener than turquoise.
It is loaded with sycamore figs, redder than jasper.
Its branches are like turquoise, their skin like faience.
Its wood is the colour of felspar. . . .
It attracts the destitute,
its shade cools the breeze.
It sends a message by hand of a maid,
the daughter of its chief gardener.

It tells her to hurry to her beloved, saying,
'Come, spend a moment among the maidens.
the meadow is in its day,
there is a canopy and a tent below me.
My servants rejoice and jubilate at seeing you.
Send your servants ahead, loaded with their equipment.
They are drunk running towards me
without yet having drunk.

65. *Wall-painting in the tomb of
Neferhotep (No. 49) at Thebes.
18th dyn.*

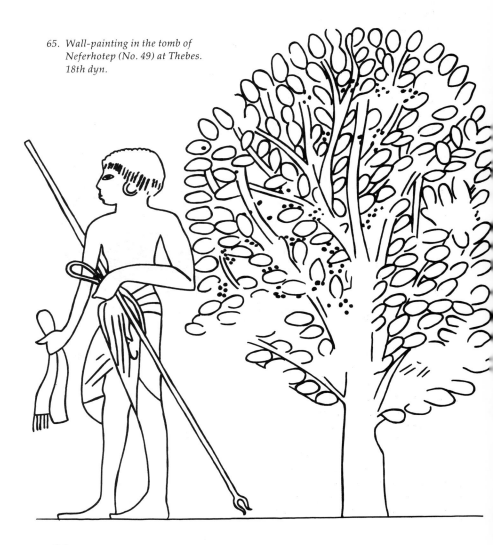

The servants of yours
have come with their provisions,
beer and loaves of bread,
herbs and bouquets from yesterday and today,
all kinds of pleasing fruits.
Come, spend the day in happiness,
day after day, three days perhaps
sitting in my shade with your friend on your right.
She lets him get drunk and does whatever he says.
The beer cellar becomes more and more drunk,
but she stays behind with her brother.
Her garment is below me,
the sister is moving about.
But I keep silent and shall not reveal what I see,
nor what their lips speak.'

66. Ostrakon from Deir el-Medina, Museo Egizio, Turin 7052. New Kingdom.

Flowers provided the inspiration for the following set of poems which rely heavily on a play of words which cannot be rendered in English. The manuscript is Papyrus Harris 500, written around 1300 BC.[41]

The purslane in the garden:
My heart like yours longs* to do for you
whatever it desires, whenever I am in your arms.
My desire is like eyepaint to my eye:
when I see you, brightness comes to my eyes.
So I come closer to look at you,
you the great one of my heart.
How beautiful is this hour!
An hour out of eternity flowed to me,
while I slept with you.
You have uplifted my heart.
Come sorrow, come joy,
Do not ever be far from me!

67. *Fayence tile, Egyptian
    Museum, Cairo JE
    89483. 19th dyn.*

The chaste trees in the garden:
One is magnified† in their presence.
I am your sister, the favourite.
Look, I am like the field which I planted with *hurer*-plants
and all kinds of sweet-smelling herbs.
How sweet is the canal in it which you dug with your own hand
for us to be refreshed by the breeze,
a lovely place to wander.

* *mekhamekha* – 'purslane'; *mekha* – 'to be equal with'.

† *s'amu* – 'chaste tree'; *s'a* – 'to enlarge'.

Your hand is in my hand,
my body trembles with joy,
my heart is exalted
because we walk together.
To hear your voice is like pomegranate wine,
I live to hear it.
Every glance you cast at me
is more beneficial to me than food and drink.

The thyme in the garden:
I take[‡] your garlands
when you come home drunk
to sleep in your bed.
I caress your thighs. . . .
(Here the scroll breaks off (Recto, 7).)

Happy, uncomplicated love is described in a number of poems, the lovers always making full use of their senses, watching, smelling, touching the beloved one. A large ostrakon (flake of limestone) now in the Cairo Museum was used to preserve for posterity the words of the poet (Cairo 25218). There is a smaller, matching fragment in the Institut français d'archéologie orientale in Cairo.

I see my sister coming.
My heart rejoices,
my arms open to embrace her.
My heart is joyful in its place,
like . . . for ever.
Do not be far.
Come to me, my mistress.

When I embrace her
and her arms are open,
I feel like a man in incense land
who is immersed in scent.
When I kiss her
and her lips are open
I rejoice
without even having drunk beer.
(IFAO 1266 + Cairo 25218, 15–6)

[‡] *zaiti* – 'thyme'; *zau* – 'take off'.

68. *Ostrakon from Deir el-Medina, Museo Egizio, Turin Suppl. 9547. 20th dyn.*

O my god, my lotus flower! . . .
It is lovely to go out and . . .
I love to go and bathe before you.
I allow you to see my beauty
in a dress of the finest linen,
drenched with fragrant unguent.
I go down into the water to be with you
and come up to you again with a red fish,
looking splendid on my fingers.
I place it before you. . . .
Come! Look at me!
(IFAO 1266 + Cairo 25218, 7–11)[42]

To appreciate the finer points of this last poem it must be realized
that the Egyptians were fascinated by the partly clothed body of a
woman. They were so used to seeing naked or semi-naked persons
around that this sight had lost its attraction and mysterious allure.
But a woman dressed in a garment of fine linen, wet and clinging
and semi-transparent, stirred their imagination. A fish had phallic
connotations and the image of this beautiful woman carrying a red
fish is full of eroticism. It is perhaps one of the most sensuous love
poems from ancient Egypt.

True love is inseparable from its twin, unfulfilled love, the anguish
and longing to be part of the life of the loved one. The Egyptians
experienced the same urge, as expressed in these poems of varying
date.

The villa of my sister, its gate is at the front.
The doors are open, the bolt is drawn.
My sister comes out angry.

I wish I were her doorkeeper
so that at least she would nag me.
Then I might hear her voice, though angry,
like a child fearing her.
(P. Harris 500 II, 11–3)[43]

O my beautiful one,
I wish I were part of your affairs, like a wife.
With your hand in mine your love would be returned.
I implore my heart:
'If my true love stays away tonight,
I shall be like someone already in the grave.'
Are you not my health and my life?
How joyful is your good health
for the heart that seeks you!
(P. Harris 500 V, 3–6)[44]

I wish I were her Nubian slave
who guards her steps.
Then I would be able to see the colour
of all her limbs!

69. *Ostrakon from Deir el-Medina,*
    Cairo IFAO 3787. New Kingdom.

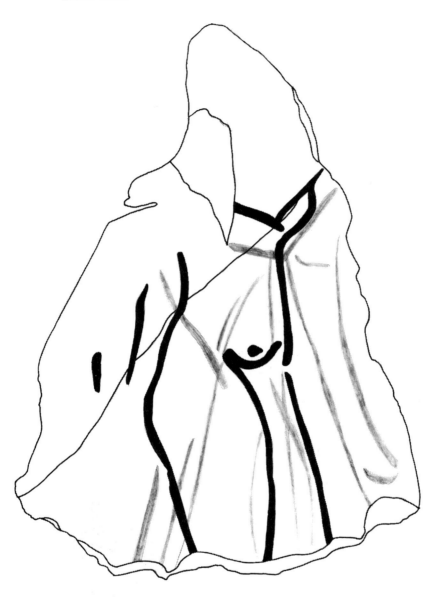

70. Ostrakon from Deir el-Medina, Museo Egizio, Turin 5639. 19th dyn.

I wish I were her laundryman,
just for a single month.
Then I would flourish by donning [her garment]
and be close to her body.
I would wash away the unguent from her clothes
and wipe my body in her dress. . . .
I wish I were the signet ring
which guards her finger,
then I would see her desire every day.
(IFAO 1266 + Cairo 25218, 18–21)[45]

I wish I were your mirror
so that you always looked at me.
I wish I were your garment
so that you would always wear me.
I wish I were the water that washes your body.
I wish I were the unguent, O woman,
that I could anoint you.
And the band around your breasts,
and the beads around your neck.
I wish I were your sandal
that you would step on me!

This last poem, so much in the Egyptian tradition, has been translated from the Greek. It is from a collection of poems by Anakreon who lived in the 6th century BC.[46] It is tempting to see in it a translation from an Egyptian original.

Love has its side-effects: compared with the kisses of the loved one, all other things are bitter:

When I see sweet cakes
they are like salt,
and pomegranate wine,
before so sweet in my mouth,
is like the gall of birds.
The scent of your nose alone
is what keeps me alive.
What I have found,
may Amun give it for ever and ever!
(P. Harris 500 V, 1–3)[47]

Figurine, British Museum.

Love may appear disguised as illness. We can imagine the young man retiring to dream and suffer for his loved one:

I will go and lie down indoors
and pretend to be ill.
The neighbours will come and see me,
and my sister will come with them.
She will make fools(?) of the doctors,
for she knows the nature of my disease.
(P. Harris 500 V, 9–11)[48]

Being with the object of one's desire was the most important thing in the world:

I found my beloved in his bed.
My heart was exceedingly happy.
We said, 'I shall never leave you.
My hand is in your hand.
I walk with you. I am with you
in all lovely places.'
He has placed me foremost among all the women.
He will never break my heart.
(P. Harris 500 V, 7–8)[49]

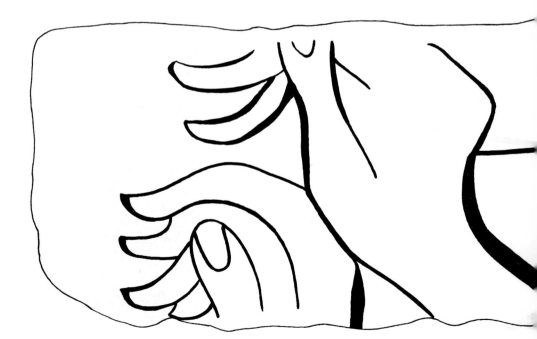

But sometimes danger lurked to separate the lovers, perhaps in the person of an angry parent. After an obscure couplet mentioning the lust of the young man, the girl asserts her opinion:

I shall not leave him,
even if they beat me . . .
and I had to spend the day in the swamp,
or if they chase me to Syria with clubs,
or to Nubia with palm ribs,
or to the desert with sticks,
or to the coast with reeds.
I will not listen to their plans
of giving up the man I love.
(P. Harris 500 II, 2–5)[50]

*71. Relief from a chapel of
    Akhnaten at Karnak. 18th dyn.*

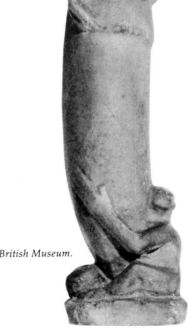

Erotic amulet, British Museum.

93

A lovers' quarrel is the subject of another poem. The young man is preparing to go home after the rendez-vous, and we can imagine the girl objecting, sourly at first, until she thinks of a way of delaying his departure.

> If you were not with me
> to whom would you give your heart?
> If you could not embrace me. . . .
> If you seek to caress my thighs. . . .
> Are you leaving because you remember food?
> Are you a slave of your stomach?
> Are you getting up for your clothes?
> But I have a sheet here!
> Are you leaving because of hunger or thirst?
> Take my breast! It overflows for you. It is all yours!
> Sweet is the day of your embrace.
> (P. Harris 500 I, 1–6)[51]

72. *Wall-painting from a
    Theban tomb,
    Ägyptisches Museum,
    East Berlin 18534.
    18th dyn.*

Maybe one day the affair came to an end, and one of the two was
left with a broken heart.

I turned my face towards the door,
for I was waiting for my brother to come to me.
My eyes were in the street, my ears listening. . . .
I was waiting for Pamehy.
All that matters is my love for my brother.
Because of him my heart will not be quiet.
He sends me a messenger
who hurries to come and go,
saying that he has betrayed me.
Admit it then! You have found another
who makes eyes at you.
Why must the ruses of another make me a stranger?
(P. Harris 500 V, 8–12)[52]

Figurine, British Museum.

Wisdom Texts

Wisdom books are a special genre within Egyptian literature. They
consist of advice composed by a specific person, sometimes with a
particular purpose in mind. Some have to do with the behaviour of
a future king, but most concern members of the upper-middle class,
the officials of the king. Many items deal with relations between the
sexes and advise as to how men should behave towards women. In
Egypt, as elsewhere, there were three kinds of women: wives, mothers
and prostitutes. A great number of the entries may still apply in
modern Western society, and they reveal something about the relations between the sexes in ancient times.

95

73. Detail of a statue group in Ägyptisches Museum, West Berlin 12547. 5th dyn.

The wisdom texts were copied in the schools of scribes through the ages. A letter from the Ramessid period suggests what some of the students were told to copy: 'The learned scribes made not unto themselves pyramids of bronze. Books of instructions became their pyramids, and the reed pen was their child. The surface of the stone was their woman. . . .' (P. Chester Beatty IV, verso)[53]

The wisdom book of Ptahhotpe

These texts have been handed down on a number of papyri, the oldest scroll among them dating from *c.* 1900 BC. The author is said to be Ptahhotpe, a vizir who lived about 600 years earlier. One piece of advice of his was quoted on p. 00, concerning what a man was to abstain from. Ptahhotpe suggests the following instead:

> If you are a wise man, establish a home and love your wife. Fill her belly, clothe her back. Ointment is a good remedy for her limbs. Make her happy as long as you live. She is a good field to her master. (323–30)[54]

The wisdom book of Ani

Ani, the scribe, wrote a wisdom book for his son around 1450 BC. The surviving manuscripts, however, are all about 200 years later.

> Take a wife while you are young that you may beget a son and she can bear him while you are still young. Happy is the man who has offspring and a large family. He is respected because of his children.
> Do not watch over your wife in her house when you know how efficient she is.
> Do not say to her, 'Where is it? Bring it!' when she has put it in its proper place.
> Let your eye observe and be silent, and you shall know her good qualities and how happy she is when you are behind her.
> A married man who has established a household must conquer his impatience.
> Go not after a woman, and let her not steal your heart.
> Beware of a strange woman who is not known in town. Do not look at her, do not know her. She is a deep pool whose swirling is not known. 'Am I not beautiful?' a woman who is far from her husband tells you every day, when no one else listens, and then she tightens the rope. (VI, 1–3 and IX, 3–7)[55]

The wisdom book of Ankhsheshonk

The author of this collection of texts was a priest who composed them while he was in prison suspected of conspiring against the king. The manuscript is no. 10,508 in the British Museum, copied shortly before the Christian era, but Ankhsheshonk lived several hundred years earlier.[56]

> Do not send a low woman on any errand of yours. She will go after her own.
> Do not marry a woman whose husband is alive, or he will become your enemy.
> Let your wife see your wealth, but do not trust her with it.
> Do not open your heart to your wife. What you have said ends up in the street.
> Do not open your heart to your wife or your sevant. Open it to your mother. She is a woman [to be trusted].
> Teaching a woman is like having a sack of sand whose side is split open.
> What a woman does with her husband today, she does with another man tomorrow.
> Do not take a young man for your companion.
> It is waste of a woman not to know her.
> When a man smells of myrrh, his wife is a cat in his presence.
> When a man is suffering, his wife is a lioness in his presence.
> A woman who is loved, when one abandons her she is really abandoned.
> Do not insult a woman whose husband is your subordinate.
> Give a hundred silver pieces to a prudent woman. Do not accept two hundred from a foolish one.
> Do not rejoice over your wife's beauty. Her mind is on her lover.
> He who is ashamed to sleep with his wife will not have children.
> He who rapes a married woman on the bed will have his own wife raped on the ground.
> He who makes love to a woman of the street will have his purse cut open on its side.
> Do not make love to a married woman.

74. Fayence figurine, British Museum.

He who makes love to a married woman is killed on her doorstep.

Man is more anxious to copulate than a donkey. What restrains him is his purse.

A good woman of noble character is food which comes in times of hunger.

May the heart of a wife be like the heart of her husband that they may be free from quarrel.

If a woman does not desire the property of her husband, she has fallen in love with another man.

A bad woman will never find a husband.

Other wisdom texts

A papyrus scroll in Leiden contains a set of wisdom texts copied during the first century AD, but composed at least a hundred years earlier. The beginning of the scroll, including the author's name, is lost. Fragments of the same texts are in Copenhagen (P. Insinger and P. Carlsberg).[57]

Do not have relations with a woman who has relations with your superior. If she is beautiful, keep away from her.

There are men who dislike intercourse, yet spend a fortune on women.

A wise man can be harmed by the woman he loves.

He who is abstemious with his belly and sparing with his phallus will never be to blame.

The fool who looks at a woman is like a fly on blood.

The fool's love of fornication harms his career.

If a woman is beautiful you must show her that you are superior.

A good woman who does not love another man in her family is a wise woman.

The women who follow these instructions are rarely bad.

There are women who fill their house with wealth without there being an income.

There are men who forget their wives when they are young because they love other women.

She is not a good woman who is pleasing to another man.

It is in women that good fortune and bad fortune are in this world.

He who is abstemious with his phallus, his name does not stink.

One does not ever discover the heart of a woman more than one does the sky.

A fool who has no work, his phallus does not let him rest.

He who is over sixty, for him everything is over. If he loves wine he can no longer drink enough to get drunk. If he loves food he can no longer eat as he used to. If he loves a woman, her moment does not come.

Wine, women and food bring joy to the heart.

He who enjoys any of the above without shouting is not reproached in the street. He who is deprived of any of it becomes an enemy of his body.

Calendars and Dream Books

The wisdom books advised as to how to behave in society in general. For more specific guidance the Egyptians were able to consult other works telling them how to behave in another town, where customs were perhaps different, or on the various days of the year. If a man or a woman had had a particular dream, dream books would provide the answer.

A papyrus found in the Delta city of Tanis[58] spoke of prohibitions in a number of towns at various times of the year, a useful guide for someone travelling to an unfamiliar destination. On the 23rd day of the third month of inundation (9 October) there was a sexual taboo: ≋ ⌐≋ ⌐ ᵚ₎ which may be translated as 'fornicating with a fornicator, male or female', i.e., having relations with prostitutes of either sex. A similar inscription was carved on a wall of the temple of Edfu in Upper Egypt: 'having intercourse with a prostitute, over the entire country'.

Calendars of lucky and unlucky days concern ordinary activities of daily life, but few of the entries deal with sexual matters. On Papyrus Sallier IV recto (BM 10184) the following may be noted:

> Day 7, 1st month of winter [22 November]. Very bad. Do not have intercourse with any woman in front of the eye of Horus [the sun]. Keep and make to burn brightly the fire which is in your house on this day.
>
> Day 5, 2nd month of summer [22 August]. Very bad. Do not leave your house on this day. Do not embrace any woman. On this day the Ennead was created. The god Monthu rested on this day. He who is born on this day shall die during intercourse.[59]

Two dream books have survived from ancient Egypt. One is written for men, the other for women. The former is to be found in Papyrus Chester Beatty III recto (BM 10683) from about 1175 BC. A series of dreams is listed, following the introductory phrase: 'If a man sees himself in a dream. . . .' Some of the dreams are erotic.

> . . . his phallus becoming large: Good. It means that his possessions will multiply.
> . . . having intercourse with his mother: Good. His companions will stick to him.
> . . . having intercourse with his sister: Good. It means that he will inherit something.
> . . . having intercourse with a woman: Bad. It means mourning.
> . . . having intercourse with a female jerboa: Bad. A judgement will be passed against him.
> . . . seeing his phallus erect: Bad. It means that he will be robbed.
> . . . having intercourse with a kite: Bad. It means that he will be robbed.

75. *Phallic figure on horseback from Saqqara.*

... shaving his lower parts: Bad. It means mourning.

... seeing a woman's vulva: Bad. The utmost misery upon him.

... having intercourse with a pig: Bad. He will be deprived of his possessions.

... having intercourse with his wife in the sun: Bad. The god will see his miseries.[60]

101

The dream book composed for women is written on Papyrus Carlsberg XIII in Copenhagen from the second century AD. As we have just seen, the tradition of dream books goes much further back in time. The papyrus scroll is somewhat damaged, but a number of interesting erotic combinations remain along with the heading:

The manners of intercourse to be dreamt of when a woman dreams

If a woman dreams that she is married to her husband, she will be destroyed. If she embraces him, she will experience grief.

If a mouse has intercourse with her, her husband will give her [lacuna].

If a horse has intercourse with her, she will use force against her husband.

If a peasant has intercourse with her, a peasant will give [lacuna].

If a donkey has intercourse with her, she will be punished for a great sin.

If a he-goat has intercourse with her, she will die soon.

If a ram has intercourse with her, Pharaoh will be benevolent towards her.

If a wolf has intercourse with her, she will see something beautiful.

If a serpent has intercourse with her, she will have a husband who will be severe(?) towards her, and she will become ill.

If a crocodile has intercourse with her, she will die soon.

If a baboon has intercourse with her, she will be benevolent towards people.

If an ibis has intercourse with her, she will have a well-equipped house.

If a falcon has intercourse with her, she will have a [lacuna] fate.

If a bird has intercourse with her, a rival of hers will gain something.

If a married woman has intercourse with her, she will have an ill fate, and one of her children will [lacuna].

If a barbarian has intercourse with her, she will take her husband, and she will be found dead.

If a Syrian has intercourse with her, she will weep, for she will let her slaves have intercourse with her.

If a foreigner(?) has intercourse with her, she will weep, for she will bear false witness. She will be friendly to those who come to her, and her husband will take another wife.

Erotic amulet, British Museum.

Erotic amulet, British Museum.

If an unknown person has intercourse with her, people will look for her without finding her.

If her(?) son has intercourse with her, one of her sons will perish.

If a female has intercourse with her, she will lie.[61]

Magical Texts

Many aspects of sexual life have come to light in the tales, the factual books and in the poems. Not everybody was happy with the state of affairs in courtship and lovemaking. Sometimes they wanted to improve on the situation or, if an enemy was concerned, make it worse. From the most ancient times magic came to the assistance of man in erotic matters. Any picture possessed a magic force which worked in daily life as well as in the Hereafter. A deceased man was given a concubine figure to accompany him, stimulate his virility and ensure his rebirth. If an Egyptian had problems concerning the former while he was yet among the living, something could certainly be done about it. A papyrus from the end of the Middle Kingdom (*c.* 1700 BC) prescribes the following poultice for impotence: 'Leaves of Christ thorn, 1; leaves of acacia, 1; honey, 1. Grind (the leaves) in this honey, and apply as a bandage.' (P. Ram. V No. XII)[62].

Medical treatment was often accompanied by magic formulas. A papyrus written around 1000 BC includes recipes for love potions. Unfortunately, it is very fragmentary. One of the remedies was to be applied while a spell was recited, most appropriately alluding to Khnum (one of the gods of creation who did not, however, create by means of his phallus, but on a potter's wheel!).

> Hail to thee, great(?) god, who created the upper class, thou Khnum who established the lower class. Mayst thou test(?) the mouth of every vulva . . . be erect, be not soft. be strong, be not weak. . . . Thou strengthenest thy testicles(?) with Seth, son of Nut. To be recited over . . . the member to be anointed with it. (P. Chester Beatty X)[63]

103

Better preserved formulas are to be found later, but their origins can be traced back in time. A papyrus written as late as the 3rd century AD contains a prescription for aphrodisiacs of various kinds. Part of the scroll is in the British Museum (no. 10070), part in Leiden (J. 383).

Love potion to win a woman's love. Take dandruff from the scalp of a dead person, who was murdered, and seven grains of barley, buried in the grave of a dead man, and crush it with 10 *oipe* of apple pips. Add the blood of a tick from a black dog, a drop of blood from the ring finger of your left hand and your semen. Crush it to a compact mass, place it in a cup of wine and add 3 *outeh mut* which you have not yet tasted and which has not yet been used for offering. Recite the said formula over it seven times and let the woman drink it. Tie the skin of the tick in a piece of linen and tie it in a knot round your left arm.

How to make a woman love her husband. Grind acacia seeds with honey, rub your phallus with it and sleep with the woman.

How to force a woman to enjoy intercourse. Rub your phallus with the foam of the mouth of a stallion and sleep with the woman.

How to separate a man from a woman, and a woman from her husband. 'Alas, alas! Fire, fire! Having transformed himself to a bull, Geb slept with his mother's daughter Tefenet again and again. His father's heart grew angry with him. The rage of the one whose soul is fire and whose body is a column flooded the entire country with fire, so that the mountains spat fire. The wrath of all gods and goddesses . . . may it come over NN, son of NN, and NN, daughter of NN. Send fire to his heart and flames to his bedroom! Kindle the glow of hate in his heart, until he expels NN, daughter of NN from his house. May she raise the anger in his heart! May she seem repulsive to him! Instigate complaints, curses, grief and endless quarrelling between them until one parts from the other never to be reconciled!'

Gum, . . . , myrrh, and wine, shape a figure of Geb with a sceptre in his hand.[64]

Erotic amulet, British Museum.

Erotic amulet, British Museum.

Some 2000 years earlier another woman had used a slightly less dramatic remedy to avenge a rival. A papyrus from around 1700 BC includes prescriptions for excess hair. One of them is for an unexpected purpose: 'Another remedy to make hair fall out: burnt lotus leaves are to be steeped in oil and placed on the head of a hated woman. (P. Ebers 475)[65]

Erotic activities in the Hereafter were stimulated by reciting a description of ideal situations or by placing the relevant text in the coffin of the deceased. In the Old Kingdom the king benefited from the Pyramid Texts[66] on his travels in the Hereafter. They were inscribed on the walls of the burial chamber inside the pyramid. The king was to be united with the goddess Isis:

> Your sister Isis come to you, rejoicing over your desire.
> You place her on your phallus.
> Your semen enters her being efficient like Sirius.*
> (Chapter 366, 1. 632 a–d)

In the Middle Kingdom (*c.* 2133–1786 BC) the texts were used by private individuals in their coffins. One of these Coffin Texts[67] runs as follows: 'Concerning every man who knows the (formula), he will be able to copulate on this earth at night and at day, and the hearts of women will come to him at any time he desires.' (426)

Another contemporary text mentions 'Bebo's phallus' which was to be procured for the deceased to give him special protection: 'The phallus of Bebo that engenders children and created calves shall be brought to the deceased. "Where shall they place it?" On the thighs, where the legs open.' (Urkunden V 156, 6ff.)[68]

This Bebo was a god who lived with the Ennead, but he was their *enfant terrible* and opposed even the mighty sun-god. When once he disobeyed Thoth, god of magic, he soon found reason to regret it.

---

* A play on words again: efficient – 'spd'; Sirius – 'spdt'.

Once again Bebo began to speak evil of Thoth, and Thoth went up to him, and when Bebo was having intercourse with a certain woman and was asleep, Thoth anointed his phallus and recited a magic formula against him. In this way Bebo's phallus became stuck in the vulva of this woman. Bebo was ignorant that his phallus had been removed. Then Thoth called the Ennead and showed them Bebo and the woman. Then Re said, 'You have lost, Bebo.' And Thoth said to Bebo, 'You great one, your testicles are far away.' Then Bebo approached Thoth with his war weapons. But Thoth pronounced his magic formulas, and as Bebo took his bronze weapon, he hit his own head. The gods said, 'His weapon is in him!' And thus his name existed to this day. The gods said, 'Punish him, O Re!' And Re placed Bebo in Thoth's power, and Thoth sacrificed him on the slaughtering ground of Re. (P. Jumilhac XVI, 15–21)[69]

Erotic amulet, British Museum.

An Erotic Cartoon[70]

One day around the year 1150 BC a draughtsman at Thebes in Upper Egypt was busy working at a scroll of papyrus. First he drew illustrations to the animal tales he knew. When he had finished, he drew a vertical line from top to bottom of the scroll and started on another subject. The illustrations to a new story which went around town? Or perhaps it was true what they said, it was something which really happened? Perhaps the characters were real people to whom he might have given names if he had wanted to?

One thing is certain. When the papyrus scroll reappeared 3000 years later these erotic drawings were subject to many interpretations and suggestions. In spite of the fact that at some stage the scribe had tried to imagine what was going on and had inserted a reconstructed dialogue wherever there was room to spare, the texts which have survived reasonably intact have not yet yielded a clue to the real significance of the pictures.

It has been suggested that the pictures represent the amorous adventure of a priest of Amun and a Theban whore, or that they were intended as an imitation of events at a higher level, in the world of the gods. Some have attempted to identify the chief male character as the king in whose reign the scroll was written.

From an artistic point of view the drawings on the scroll, including the satirical fables, have much in common with the flakes of limestone or pottery found in the workmen's village at Deir el-Medina. Considering our knowledge of the ethics in this particular place it would be an obvious place to inspire the scenes, though it must be kept in mind that similar situations must have applied to other settlements in Egypt where the evidence has not survived.

A glance at the drawings reveals that it is not one and the same man appearing in all the scenes, not only because of the different facial characteristics but also because at least one man has a few hairs remaining on his head while most of the others are more or less bald. All have different beards. They have the simple garment in common: a loosely tied kilt. All this is typical of men in the lower class, servants, filed labourers and ordinary craftsmen.

Although one girl might don different wigs it is more likely that there are several different women participating. Sometimes a lotus flower has been arranged on top of the wig but, otherwise, they wear nothing but hip belt, necklaces, armlets and, naturally, eyepaint and lip colour which one of them is shown applying with a stick.

The events take place indoors and the room is equipped with the necessary furnishings to enhance an erotic atmosphere. A bed has been prepared in a separate room; there are plenty of cushions on the floor and stools, if these are more comfortable. A lyre on the floor awaits being picked up and played to accompany the girls singing – when they have a moment to spare. The sistrum, the rattle especially devoted to Hathor, goddess of love, has also been brought. The jars are full of wine or beer, and careful search reveals objects which may add to the pleasure anticipated. When one considers the fact that almost all of those present are more or less engaged in various forms of intercourse there can hardly be any doubt that we are experiencing a unique glimpse behind the screen in a whorehouse at Deir el-Medina. Thanks to the scribe we are even allowed to overhear part of the conversation.

The text reads from right to left and, although it may not tell a continuous story, we shall read the pictures in the same direction.

III   **II**

I

The girl is bent over in a position reminiscent of that of the goddess
Nut when, during the creation of the world, she was separated from
Geb, the earth (cf. fig. 18). The man carries a sack over his shoulder
and takes her from behind.

  (She:) 'Remove(?) the bands you have placed. . . .'

II

The girl stands in a chariot drawn by two young girls. With one hand
she holds the reins while the other rests on a stem of convolvulus, a
plant frequently found in erotic contexts. (The scroll is now more
damaged than when it was found in the nineteenth century, but the
details can be see on an earlier drawing.) The man approaches her
from behind. His one hand grasps the wig of the girl, in the other
he holds a jar of ointment(?). A sistrum dangles from his arm. A little
monkey climbs on the chariot. The party is joined by a short man
who openly displays his desire.

108

I

III

The girl sits on a stool and helps her inexperienced client. The sistrum and the ointment jar(?) are on the floor – perhaps they were the same used by the triumphant neighbour? A text has been inserted over II and III and between the figures.

(The author?:) 'Look here, Thoth (god of the scribes) . . . you . . . she alone. Her second(?) [is] behind. . . . Her . . . when you have sought the heart at . . . for trembling.'

(She:) 'I make your job a pleasant one. Do not fear. What would I do to you? You . . . day, you who knocks in, you who turn around! Look here, come round behind me. [I] contain your pleasure, your phallus is with me. You have not brought me . . . lovely, my bastard!'

VI　　　　　　　　　　　　　　　　**V**

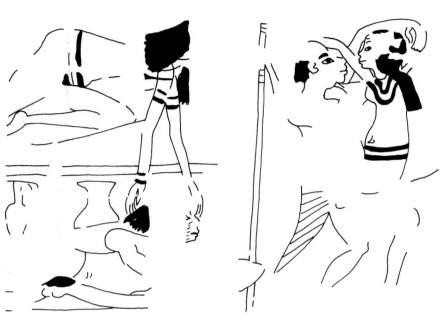

IV

The girl is making herself up in front of a mirror. She sits with legs apart on an inverted jar, while her partner looks at her and points at her vulva with his right hand. There are some illegible lines of text between this scene and the following one.

V

The couple in a tight embrace, the position known elsewhere (see fig. 57).

VI

The girl climbs on the bed while the man has been taken ill and is lying on the floor.

    (She:) 'Leave my bed alone, and I'll . . . semen(?) at me(?).'

    (He:) 'My big phallus . . . which suffers . . . inside.'

110

IV

IX   **VIII**

VII

Another client has been taken ill and is carried off by the girl and two assistants. The scroll is very damaged here, but an older drawing shows that the man's phallus, although still large, is now flaccid.

VIII

Another reminder of the 'Geb and Nut position'. The man lies on the floor while the girl supports his head. Maybe it is the same man as in VI–VIII, but in the older drawings he has different hair and beard. Four lines of text have been added between VIII and IX.

(She:) 'I'll tell you . . . pleasure . . . I . . . yours.'

IX

Intercourse from behind. The girl supports her weight on a green cushion. Like his counterpart in I the man grasps the girl's wig and has a sack over his shoulder.

VII

XII   **XI**

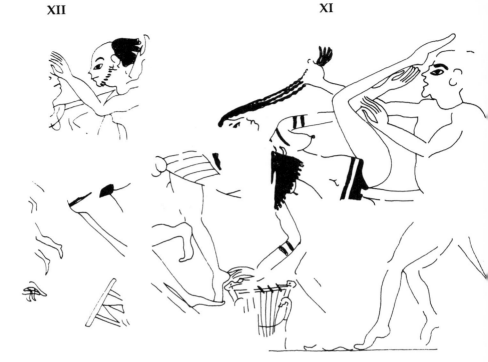

X

A very damaged scene. The girl lies on her back on a cushion with her legs around the neck of the man.

(She:) 'Take the place of the other one(?), and I'll give praise and thank(?) my god for your lust. . . .'

XI

The girl stands or lies with her legs apart next to her lyre while the man grasps her hair.

(She:) 'Praise be to god(?)'

XII

The older drawings show the girl with a brush or cosmetic stick in her right hand. The stool is overturned and the girl lies on a oblique board(?) while the man enters her. A little man runs away from the animated scene. Here the scroll comes to an end.

114

X

Epilogue

Phallic amulet, British Museum.

It is evident from the preceding pages that the Ancient Egyptians were real human beings, not only a people who built massive pyramids and made mummies of their dead. As in other early, so-called primitive civilizations erotic matters were of prime importance and became an integral part of life. This is most significantly perceived in the funerary beliefs centring around the idea of rebirth and in the sexual needs of the divinities worshipped in the temples. In this official ambience focus was on the dynamic erotic power which would cause Egyptian society to renew itself, yet remain essentially the same, like the corn sprouting in the field each summer or the eternal succession of one animal fecundating another. Creation took place once in the beginning. Re-creation was what followed.

The erotic imagination of the Egyptians was undoubtedly even more sophisticated than the sources reveal. Very few of the extant texts can be said to be of a pornographic nature, though some of the illustrations can be interpreted to that effect. But, when reading between the lines of the documents, we catch a glimpse of the Egyptians as mere mortals, falling in love, rejoicing and suffering; copulating in the little huts of crowded villages; drawing rude pictures in public places; jostling on the banks of the river or along a processional highway to see their gods and be rejuvenated; tip-toeing up to the shrine of the goddess of love to place a crudely cut votive phallus in her proximity, hoping that either virility or a child might ensue; or gathering an aphrodisiac herb in the garden to be made into a foul-tasting, but efficacious potion to cure, to prevent or to entice.

It is to be hoped that more documentation on this aspect of the life of the Ancient Egyptians will come to light in the future. It is through basic human needs, common to all people at all times, that one touches intimately the lives of an ancient people.

Erotic amulet, British Museum.

List of Illustrations

Bibliography and Notes

1 For these and the following quotations see the original text and translation by A. D. Godley, *Herodotus I–II*, Loeb Classical Library, London, 1946, and a commentary to some paragraphs in A. B. Lloyd, *Herodotus Book II. Commentary 1–98*, Leiden, 1976.

2 Papyrus Nu: E. A. W. Budge, *The Book of the Dead*, London, 1898, pp. 250–51 (hieroglyphic text) and p. 191 (translation).

3 Diodorus: Original text and translation, C. H. Oldfather, *Diodorus of Sicily*, Loeb Classical Library, London, 1968.

4 Plutarch: J. G. Griffiths, *Plutarch's De Iside et Osiride*, University of Wales Press, 1970.

5 Strabo: H. L. Jones, *The Geography of Strabo*, Loeb Classical Library, London, 1959.

6 Socle Béhague: A. Klasens, *A Magical Statue Base (Socle Béhague) in the Museum of Antiquities, Leiden*, Leiden, 1952.

7 Amenemhet: Gardiner in *Zeitschrift für ägyptische Sprache* 47, 1910, p. 92, pl. I.

8 Papyrus Leiden 371: A. H. Gardiner & K. Sethe, *Egyptian Letters to the Dead*, London, 1928, reprinted 1975.

9 Hekanakhte: T. G. H. James, *The Hekanakhte Papers and other Early Middle Kingdom Documents*, New York, 1962.

10 Papyrus Bibliothèque Nationale 198, II: J. Černý, *Late Ramesside Letters*, Bibliotheca Aegyptiaca IX, Brussels, 1939.

11 Papyrus Nestanebtasheru: see *Journal of the American Research Center in Egypt* 6, 1967, p. 99, n. 22.

12 Papyrus Carlsberg XIII: A. Volten, *Demotische Traumdeutung*, Copenhagen, 1942.

13 Curse: Spiegelberg in *Recueil de travaux relatifs à la philologie et à l'archéologie égyptienne et assyrienne* 25, 1903, p. 192.

14 Papyrus Lansing: A. H. Gardiner, *Late Egyptian Miscellanies*, Bibliotheca Aegyptiaca VII, Brussels, 1937; translation R. A. Caminos, *Late Egyptian Miscellanies*, London, 1954.

15 Tomb of Ti: W. Steindorff, *Das Grab des Ti*, Leipzig, 1913 (pl. 110).

16 For the different words to describe sexual intercourse, cf. A. Erman & H. Grapow, *Wörterbuch der ägyptischen Sprache* under the following: I. 9 *ỉpd* 'begatten'; I. 291 *wbꜣ* 'entjungfern'; I. 359 *wsn* 'begatten'; I. 459 *bnbn* 'als eine sexuelle Betätigung'; I. 497 *pꜣj* 'begatten, bespringen'; II. 81 *mnmn* 'begatten'; II. 284 *nhp* 'bespringen, begatten'; II. 345 *nk* 'den Beischlaf vollziehen'; II. 346 *nkjkj* 'den Leib der Frau befruchten?'; II. 381 *ndmndm* 'eine Frau beschlafen'; II. 446 *rḫ* 'kennen'; III. 364 *ḥꜥ* '(eine Frau) schänden'; III. 451 *smꜣ* 'begatten'; IV. 207 *shbj* '(eine Jungfrau) schänden'; IV. 347 *stj* 'Same ergiessen, begatten'; IV. 380 *sḏꜣm* 'sich geschlechtlich abgeben mit einer Frau'; IV. 391 *sḏr* 'schlafen (von Beischlaf)'; V. 419 *dꜣdꜣ* 'eine unzuchtige sexuelle Betätigung'; V. 458 *dmḏ* 'sich geschlechtlich abgeben mit einer Frau'.

17 Papyrus Chester Beatty I: A. H. Gardiner, *The Chester Beatty Papyrus No. I*, London, 1931.

18 Papyrus Kahun VI: F. L. Griffith (ed.), *Hieratic Papyri from Kahun and Gurob*, London, 1898, pl. 3, VI, 12, 28 ff., cf. J. G. Griffiths, *The Conflict of Horus and Seth from Egyptian and Classical Sources*, Liverpool, 1960, p. 42.

19 Papyrus Jumilhac III: J. Vandier, *Le Papyrus Jumilhac*, Paris, 1961.

20 Papyrus Chester Beatty: *op. cit.*

21 ibid.

22 Papyrus Jumilhac: *op. cit.*

23 Papyrus Chester Beatty: *op. cit.*

24 ibid.

25 Papyrus Kahun: *op. cit.*

26 Louvre C 286: Moret in *Bulletin de l'Institut français d'archéologie orientale*

30, 1930, pp. 725–50, cf. Desroches-Noblecourt ibid. 53, 1953, p. 19, n. 1.

27 Papyrus Louvre 3079: Spiegelberg in *Zeitschrift fur ägyptische Sprache* 53, 1917, pp. 94ff.

28 Urkunden IV: K. Sethe, *Urkunden der 18. Dynastie, historische-biografische Urkunden*, Leipzig, 1906–9.

29 Diodorus: cf. note 3.

30 Papyrus Westcar: A. Erman, *Die Märchen des Papyrus Westcar*, Berlin, 1890.

31 Papyrus d'Orbiney: A. H. Gardiner, *Late Egyptian Stories*, Bibliotheca Aegyptiaca I, Brussels, 1932, reprinted 1973, pp. 9–29; translated by M. Lichtheim, *Ancient Egyptian Literature* II, Berkeley, Los Angeles, London, 1976, pp. 203–11.

32 Papyrus Cairo 30646: F. L. Griffith, *Stories of the High Priests of Memphis* I, Oxford, 1900; more recent translation by Lichtheim, *op. cit.* III, 1980, pp. 125–38.

33 Papyrus Berlin 3024: A. H. Gardiner, *Literarische Texte des Mittleren Reiches* II, Leipzig, 1909.

34 Papyrus BM 10682: A. H. Gardiner, *Hieratic Papyri in the British Museum*, Third Series I–II, London, 1935.

35 Papyrus Westcar: cf. note 30, and L. Manniche, *How Djadja-em-ankh Saved the Day*, New York, 1976.

36 Papyrus Louvre E 25351: Posener in *Revue d'Égyptologie* 11, 1957, pp. 119–37.

37 Papyrus Chester Beatty: cf. note 17.

38 For 'The beginning of the sweet verses' cf. also Iversen in *Journal of Egyptian Archaeology* 65, 1979, pp. 78–85.

39 Papyrus Chester Beatty I, *op. cit.*

40 Papyrus Turin 1966: G. Maspero, *Les chants d'amour du Papyrus de Turin et du Papyrus Harris No. 500*, Études égyptiennes I, Paris, 1883, pp. 217ff.

41 Papyrus Harris 500: cf. n. 40 and E. A. W. Budge, *Facsimile of Egyptian Hieratic Papyri in the British Museum*, London, 1923.

42 Cairo 25218 and IFAO 1266: G. Posener, *Catalogue des ostrakas hiératiques litteraires de Deir el Médineh* II, fasc. 3, Cairo, 1972, pp. 43–44, pls. 75–79a.

43 Papyrus Harris 500: *op. cit.*

44 ibid.

45 IFAO 1266 + Cairo 25218, 18–21: *op. cit.*

46 Papyrus Anakreon: K. Preisendanz, *Anacreon. Carmina Anacreotea*, Leipzig, 1912, pp. 19ff.

47 Papyrus Harris 500: *op. cit.*

48 ibid.

49 ibid.

50 ibid.

51 ibid.

52 ibid.

53 Papyrus Chester Beatty IV: A. H. Gardiner, *Hieratic Papyri in the British Museum*, Third Series I–II, London, 1935.

54 Wisdom of Ptahhotpe: Z. Zaba, *Les Maximes de Ptaḥḥotep*, Prague, 1956.

55 Wisdom of Ani: E. Suys, *La sagesse d'Ani: Texte, traduction et commentaire*, Analecta Orientalia II, Rome, 1935.

56 Wisdom of Ankhsheshonk: S. R. K. Glanville, *Catalogue of Demotic Papyri in the British Museum* II, London, 1955, cf. Lichtheim, *op. cit.*, III, pp. 164ff.

57 Papyrus Insinger: F. Lexa, *Papyrus Insinger: Les enseignements moraux d'un scribe égyptien du premier siècle après J.-C. Texte démotique avec transcription, traduction française, commentaire, vocabulaire et introduction grammaticale et litéraire* I–II, Paris, 1926. Cf. also Lichtheim, *op. cit.*, III, pp. 184ff.

58 Papyrus Tanis: Montet in *Kêmi* 11, 1950, pp. 104–5, 112–3, 116. Edfu text: E. Chassinat, *Le temple d'Edfou* I, Cairo, 1897 (p. 330).

59 Papyrus Sallier IV: E. A. W. Budge, *Facsimile of Egyptian Hieratic Papyri in the British Museum*, London, 1923.

60 Papyrus Chester Beatty III: A. H. Gardiner, *Hieratic Papyri in the British Museum*, Third Series I–II, London, 1935.

61 Papyrus Carlsberg XIII: cf. n. 12.

62 Papyrus Ramesseum V: H. von Deines, H. Grapow & W. Westendorf, *Grundriss der Medizin der alten Ägypter*, Berlin, 1958.

63 Papyrus Chester Beatty X: A. H. Gardiner, *Hieratic Papyri in the British Museum*, Third Series I–II, London, 1935.

64 Papyrus BM 10070 and Papyrus Leiden J. 383: F. Lexa, *La magie dans l'Egypte antique* II, Paris, 1925, pp. 139 and 142.

65 Papyrus Ebers: H. von Deines, H. Grapow & W. Westendorf, *Grundriss der Medizin der alten Ägypter*, Berlin, 1958.

66 Pyramid Texts: K. Sethe, *Die altägyptischen Pyramidentexte*, Leipzig, 1909–22.

67 Coffin Texts: R. O. Faulkner, *The Ancient Egyptian Coffin Texts*, Warminster, 1973–8.

68 Urkunden V: H. Grapow, *Religiöse Urkunden* I–III, Leipzig, 1915–7.

69 Papyrus Jumilhac: Vandier in *Revue d'Égyptologie* 9, 1952, pp. 121–3.

70 Erotic cartoon: J. A. Omlin, *Der Papyrus 55001 und seine satirisch-erotischen Zeichnungen und Inschriften*, Turin, 1973.

General works not included in the Bibliography

Leca, A.-P., *La médicine égyptienne aux temps des pharaons*, Paris, 1971, ch. XXIX.

Manniche, L., 'Some Aspects of Ancient Egyptian Sexual Life', *Acta Orientalia* 38, 1977, pp. 11–23.

de Rachewiltz, B., *Black Eros*, London, 1964.

Störk, L., 'Erotik', *Lexikon der Ägyptologie* II, Wiesbaden, 1975, cols. 4–11.

Love poems

Hermann, A., *Altägyptische Liebesdichtung*, Wiesbaden, 1959.

Müller, W. M. *Die Liebespoesie der alten Ägypter*, Leipzig, 1899.

Schott, S., *Altägyptische Liebeslieder*, Zürich, 1950.

Erotic symbolism

Derchain, P., 'La perruque et le cristal', *Studien zur altägyptischen Kultur* 2, 1975, pp. 55–74.

'Le lotus, le mandragore et le perséa', *Chronique d'Égypte* 50, 1975, pp. 65–86.

'Symbols and Metaphors in Literature and Representatives of Private Life', *Royal Anthropological Institute News*, August 1976, No. 15, pp. 7–10.

Desroches-Noblecourt, C., 'Poissons, tabous et transformations du mort', *Kêmi* 13, 1954, pp. 33–42.

Westendorf, W., 'Bemerkungen zur "Kammer der Wiedergeburt" im Tutankhamun-grab', *Zeitschrift fur ägyptische Sprache* 94, 1967, pp. 139–50.

Chronology

Old Kingdom	*c.* 2686–2181 BC	
Middle Kingdom	2133–1786	
New Kingdom		
18th dynasty	1567–1320 ⎫	
19th dynasty	1320–1200 ⎬	Ramessid Period
20th dynasty	1200–1085 ⎭	
Late Period	1085–332	
Ptolemaic Period	332–31	
Roman Period	31 BC–AD 395	

Index

Page numbers in *italics* refer to illustrations